# THE BEST OF

# THE BEATLES

밴드 스코어 비틀즈 베스트

# THE BEST OF
# THE BEATLES

밴드 스코어 비틀즈 베스트

2017년 9월 1일 발행
2020년 4월 30일 2쇄 발행

**지은이** SRMUSIC 편집부

**펴낸곳** SRM(에스알엠)
**펴낸이** 하성훈
**주소** 서울시 서초구 반포대로 22길 85 에덴빌딩 3층
**등록번호** 제16-2389 · **등록일자** 2001년 4월 26일
**인터넷 홈페이지** www.srmusic.co.kr

**편집** 유제영, 김지은, 이승희
**디자인** 양은주
**마케팅** 신동수

값 29,000원
ISBN 979-11-86471-59-3

# THE BEST OF
# THE BEATLES

# CONTENTS

# I Saw Her Standing There

Words & Music by
John Lennon, Paul McCartney

1.3.
A E7
1.– se - ven - teen – You know what I mean – And the
2.– looked at me – And I, – I - could see – That be-
3.4.– through the night – And we held each o - ther tight – And be-
A7
E7
E7
way she looked was way be - yond com pare – – So
- fore too long I'd fall in love – with her – – Now
- fore too long I fell in love – with her – –
B7
Vocal
Guitar I
Guitar II
Bass
Drums

B
14
E7    E7/G#    A7    C
Vocal
Guitar I
Guitar II
Bass
Drums
how    could I    dance – with a – no – ther    Oh, – – when I
She    would-n't    dance – with a – no – ther    Oh, – – when I
I'll    ne – ver    dance – with a – no – ther    Oh, – – when I
4. (Since I)
3
3
3
0 0 0 0    4 4 4 4    5 5 5 5    3 3 3 3
7 7 7 7    6 6 6 6    7 7 7 7    5 5 5 5
18
E7    B7    to 1.3. E7    1.
Vocal
Guitar I
Guitar II
Bass
Drums
saw    her    stand – – ing there
saw    her    stand – – ing there
saw    her    stand – – ing there
Well, she-
3    3    3
0 0 4 0    2 2    5 4    2 2 2 2 2 2 2 2    0 0 4 0    2 2    5 4
7 7 6 7 9 7 7 6    7 7 6 9 7 7 6    7 7 6 7 7 9 7 7 6

22
2. E7
C A7 2.
Vocal
Well, my heart went boom – When I crossed that room – And I
Guitar I
Guitar II
Bass
Drums
27
A7
B7
held her hand – in mine – – – – – And I
Guitar I
Guitar II
Bass
Drums
S
S

31
A7    to Coda 2.
Vocal
Guitar I
Guitar II
Bass
Drums
Oh, we danced
Coda 1.
E7    B7
there Ah
D.S.1.
D
35
E7
Vocal
Guitar I
C    H+P
H    H
S
H
Guitar II
Bass
Drums
10

39
E7
B7
Vocal
Guitar I
Guitar II
Bass
Drums
E
43
E7
A7
11

47
E7    B7    E7    B7
Vocal
Guitar I
Guitar II
Bass
Drums
Well, my
D.S.2.
Coda 2.
Coda 3.
51
A7
E7
– Oh, – we danced
there        Oh, since I    saw    her
D.S.3.
12

55
B7
E7
Vocal
Guitar I
Guitar II
Bass
Drums
stand - ing there - Yeah, well, since I saw her
59
B7
A7
E7
stand - ing there
13

# Please Please Me

Words & Music by
John Lennon, Paul McCartney

Vocal
Other
Guitar I
Guitar II
Bass
Drums
B  E                           A          E        G        A        B
1.3. Last night I said these words to my - - - girl
2. You don't need me to show the way, - - - love
E                              A          E
I know you nev - er e - ven try, - - - girl
Why do I al - ways have to say, - - - love

E
A
C
Come on, –
F#m
come on, –
C#m
come on, –
12
Vocal
Other
Guitar I
T A B
Guitar II
T A B
Bass
T A B
Drums
Come on,
come on,
come on,
come
A
come on, –
E
Please, please
me, woh
A
yeah, Like I
B
please
to
E
you
1.
16
Vocal
Other
Guitar I
T A B
Guitar II
T A B
Bass
S
T A B
S
Drums
on,
Please, please
me, woh – yeah, Like I
please
you

you
you
I don't want to sound com-plain-ing, but you know there's al-ways rain in my – – – heart

26
Vocal
Other
Guitar I
Guitar II
Bass
Drums
E
A
B
E
In - my heart
Ah
ah
with you,
woh
I do all the pleas-ing with you, it's so hard to rea-son with you, woh -
3
3
3
7 7 6 9 6 7
7 9 7
9
9 9 7 6
9
7 7 6 9 6 7
30
Vocal
Other
Guitar I
Guitar II
Bass
Drums
A
B
E
A
B
yeah
Why do you make me blue?
yeah
Why do you make me blue?
9 8 6
9
6 9 6
3
3
3
3
3
7 7 7 9
9 9
7 7 6 9 6 7
7 6 9
7
D.S.
18

Coda
33
Vocal
Other
Guitar I
Guitar II
Bass
Drums
E
A
B
E
you,
woh
yeah
Like I please
you,
woh
you,
woh - yeah
Like I please
you,
woh -
S
S
36
A
B
E
G
C
B
E
yeah
Like I please
you -  -  -  -  -  -  -
yeah
Like I please
you

# Love Me Do

Words & Music by
John Lennon, Paul McCartney

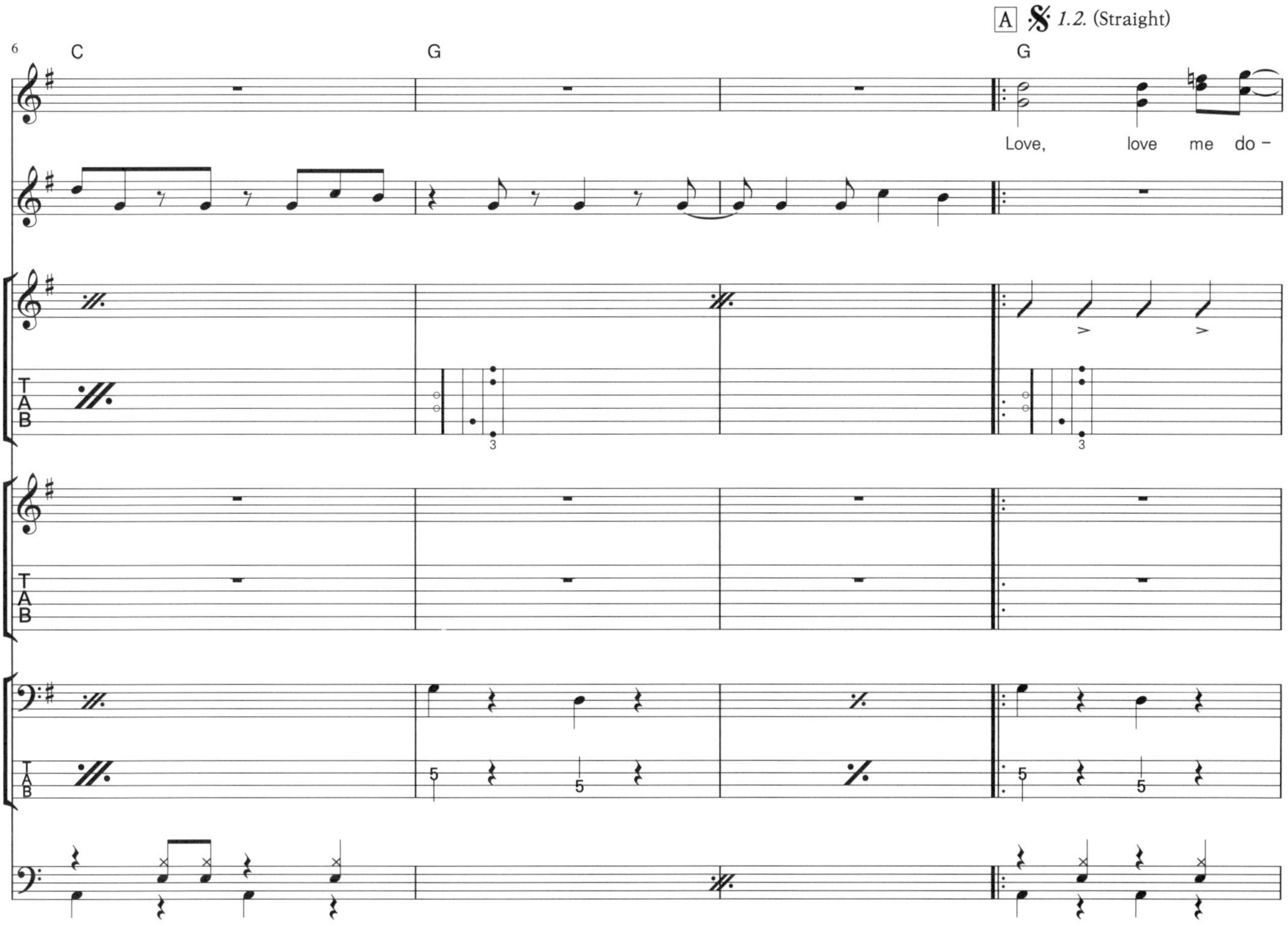
A
1.2. (Straight)
6
C
G
G
Vocal
Love, love me do –
Other
Guitar I
T A B
3
Guitar II
Bass
5
Drums

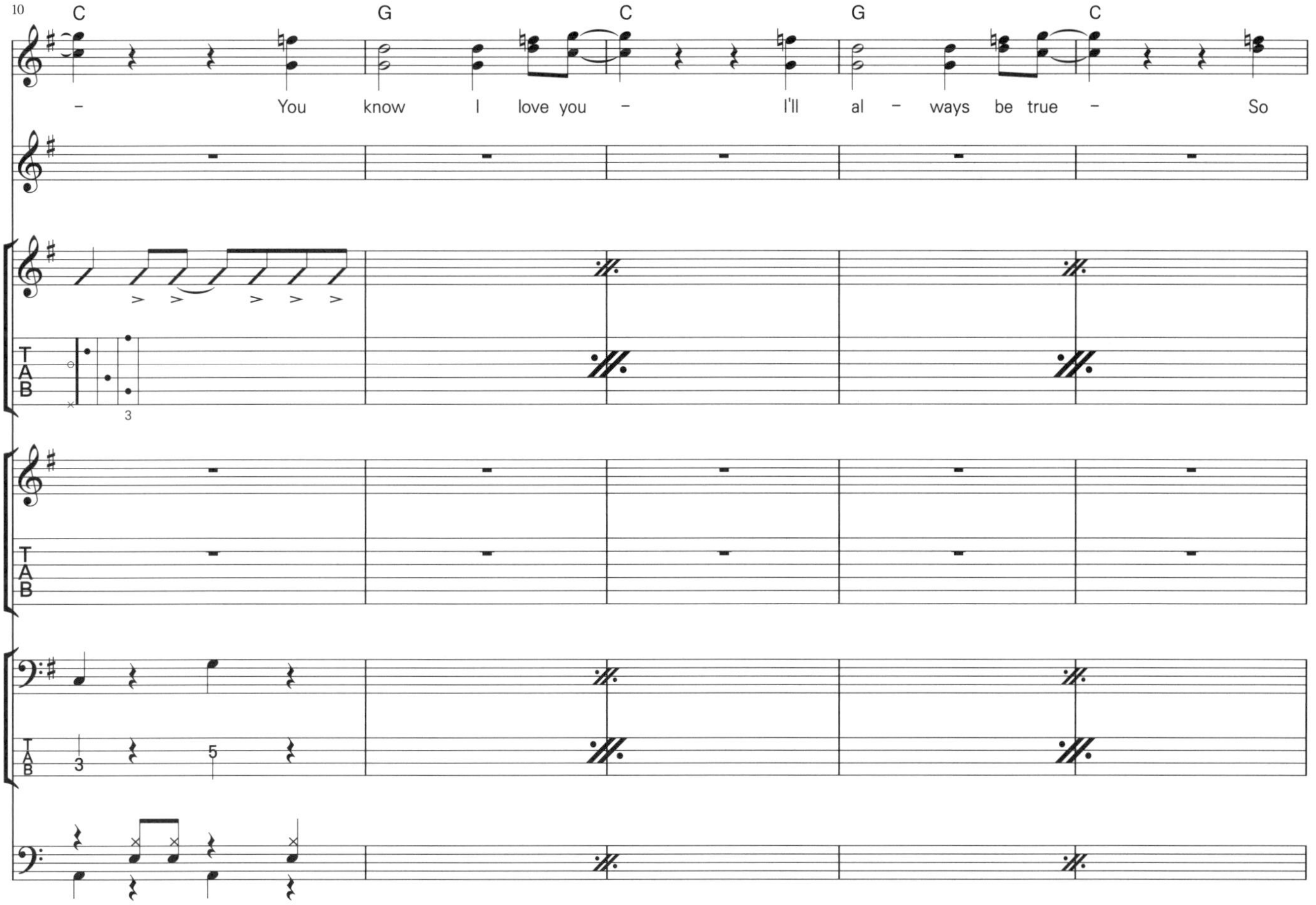
10
C
G
C
G
C
Vocal
– You know I love you – I'll al – ways be true – So
Other
Guitar I
T A B
3
Guitar II
Bass
3
5
Drums

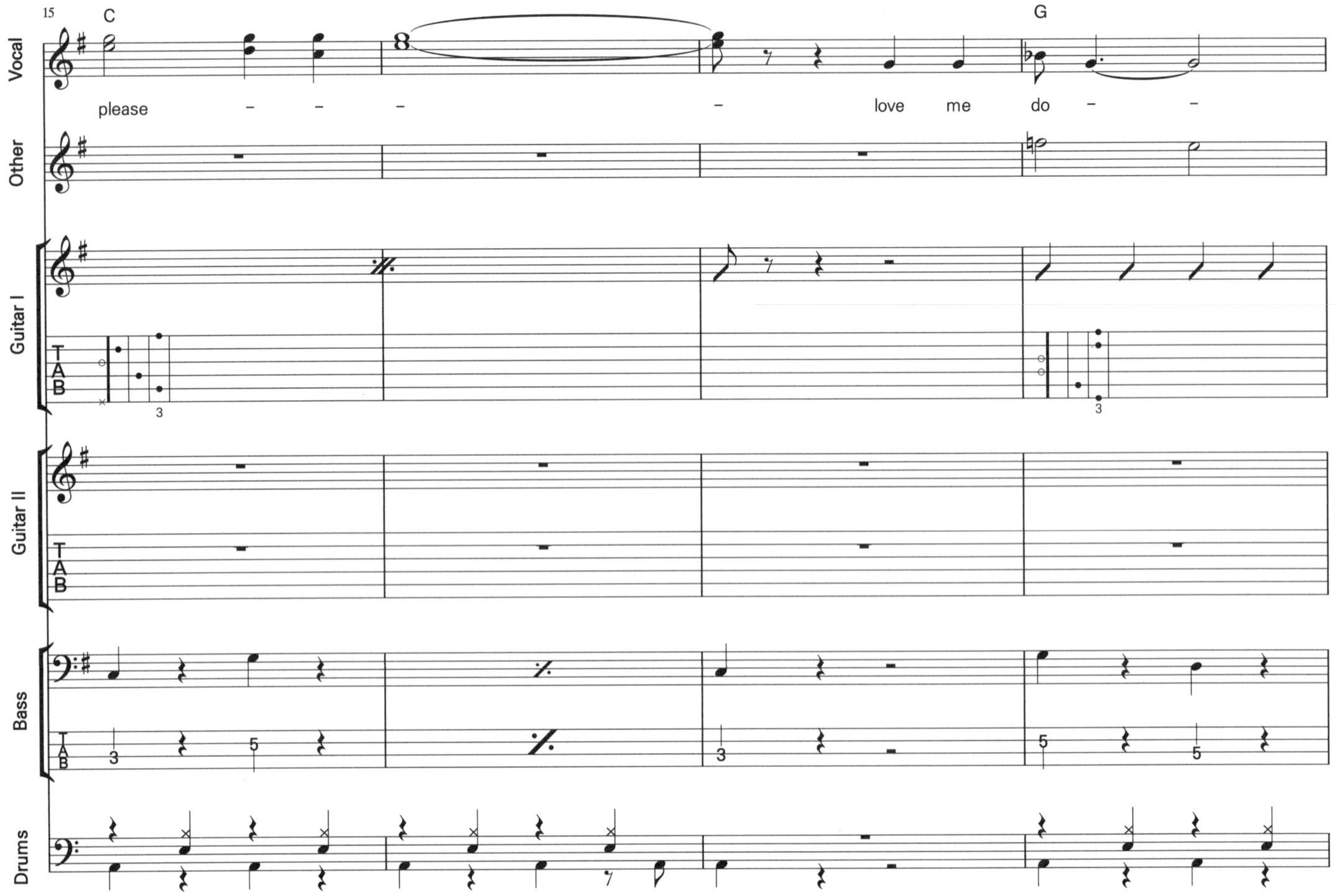
15
C
G
Vocal
please – – – – love me do – –
Other
Guitar I
Guitar II
Bass
Drums

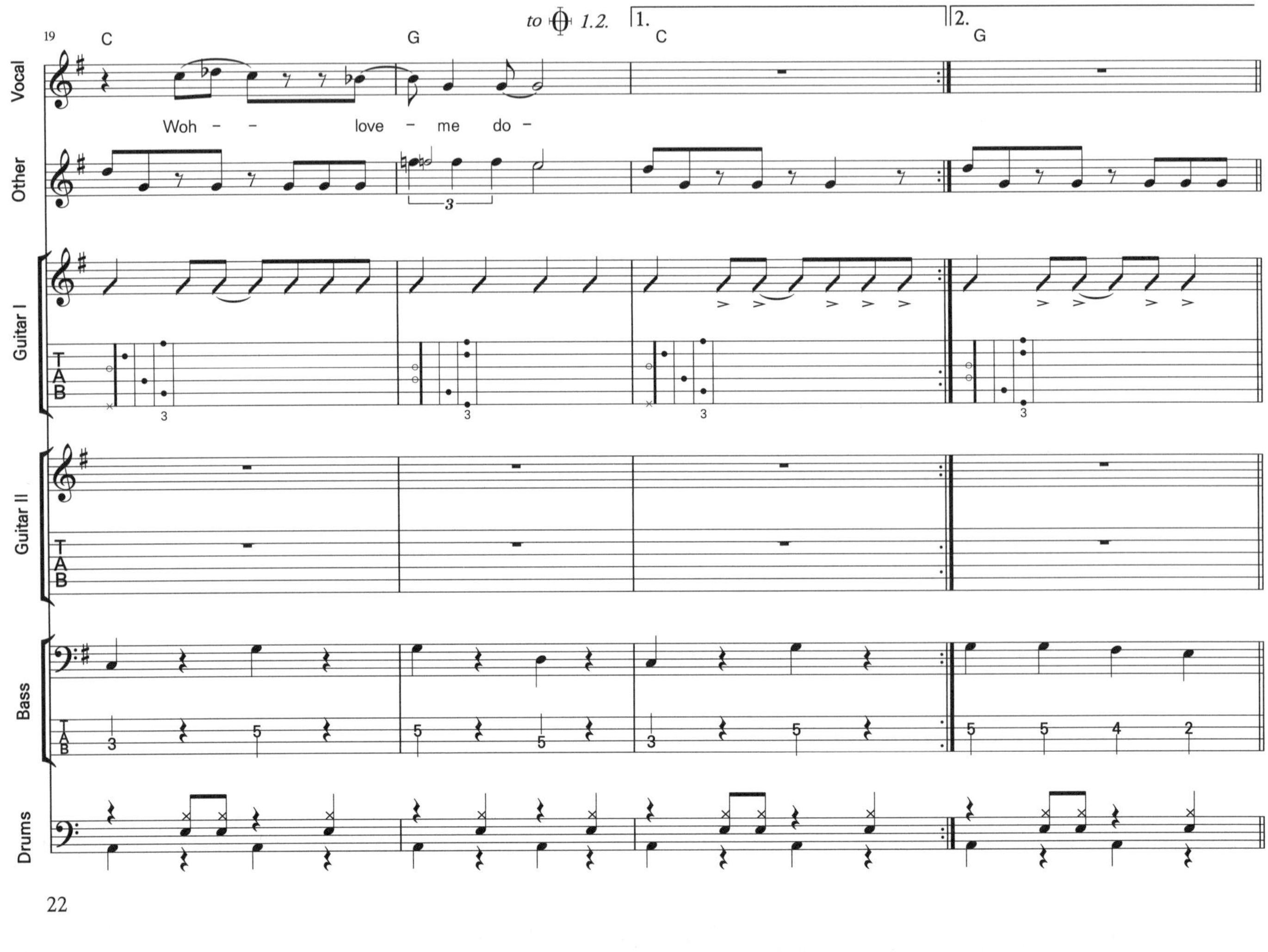
to ⊕ 1.2.
1.
2.
19
C
G
C
G
Vocal
Woh – – love – me do –
Other
Guitar I
Guitar II
Bass
Drums

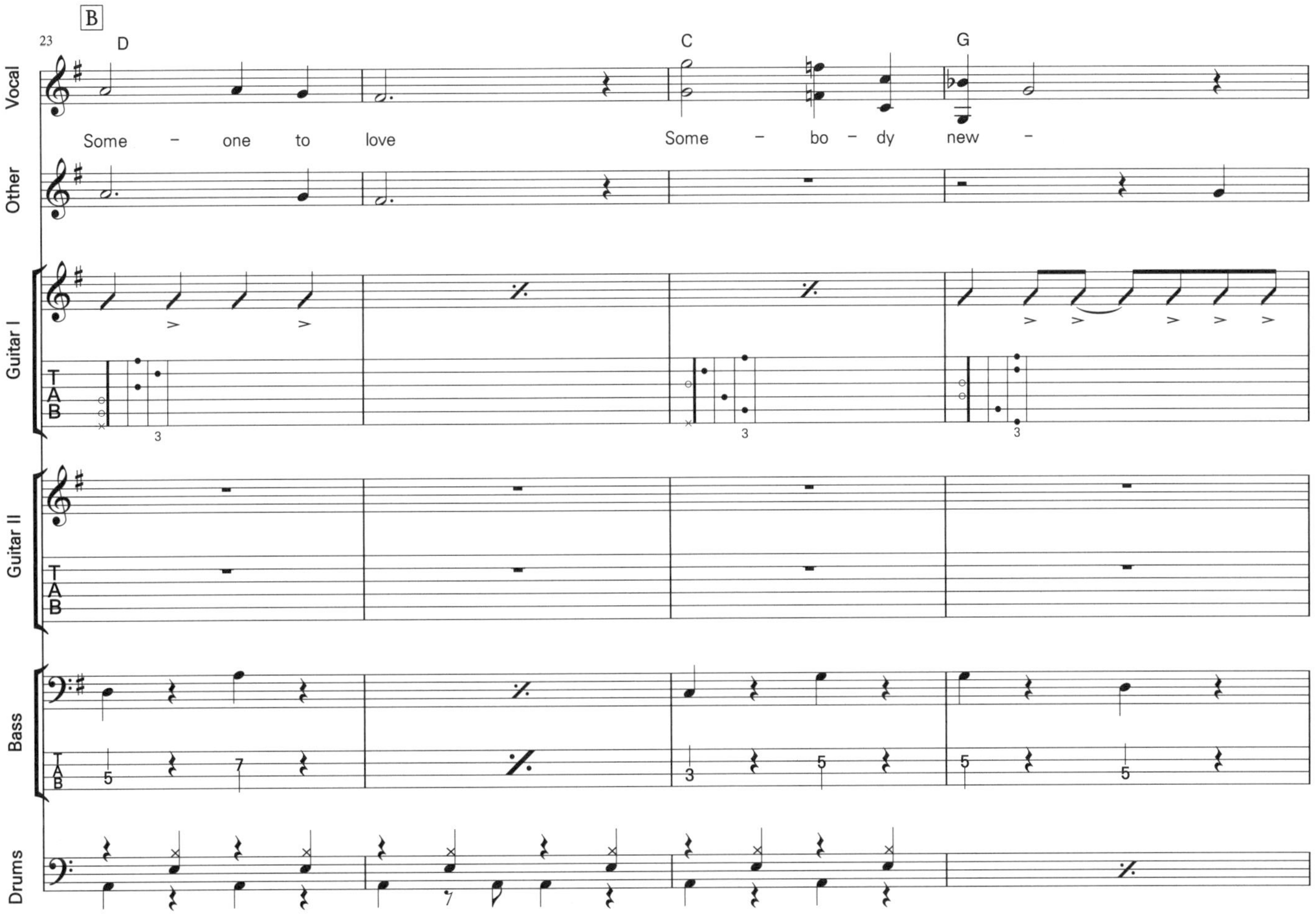
B
23
D
C
G
Vocal
Some – one to love
Some – bo – dy new –
Other
Guitar I
Guitar II
Bass
Drums

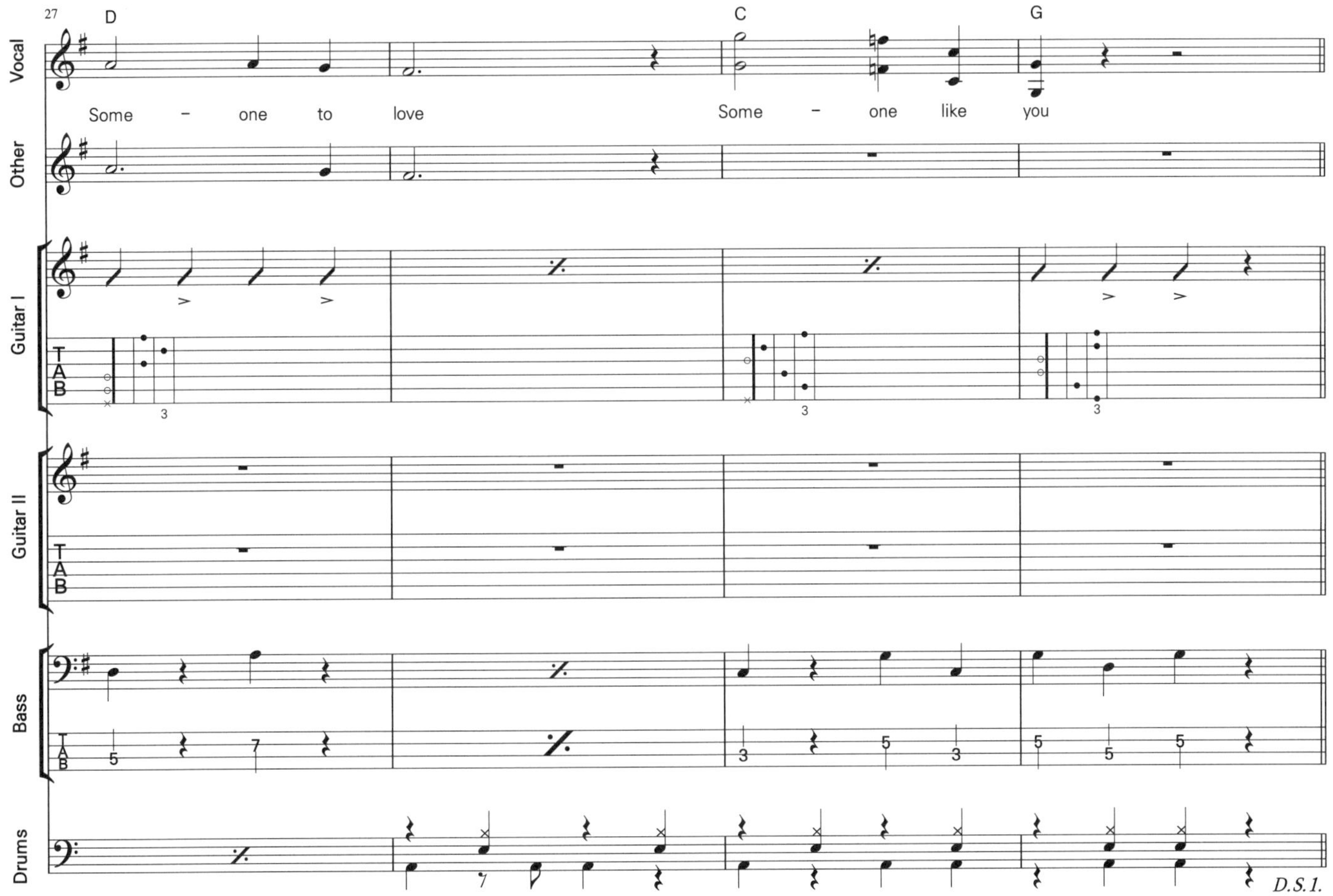
27
D
C
G
Vocal
Some – one to love
Some – one like you
Other
Guitar I
Guitar II
Bass
Drums
D.S.1.

Coda 1.
31
C
G
D
C
Vocal
Other
Guitar I
Guitar II
Bass
Drums
35
G
D
C
Vocal
Other
Guitar I
Guitar II
Bass
Drums
24

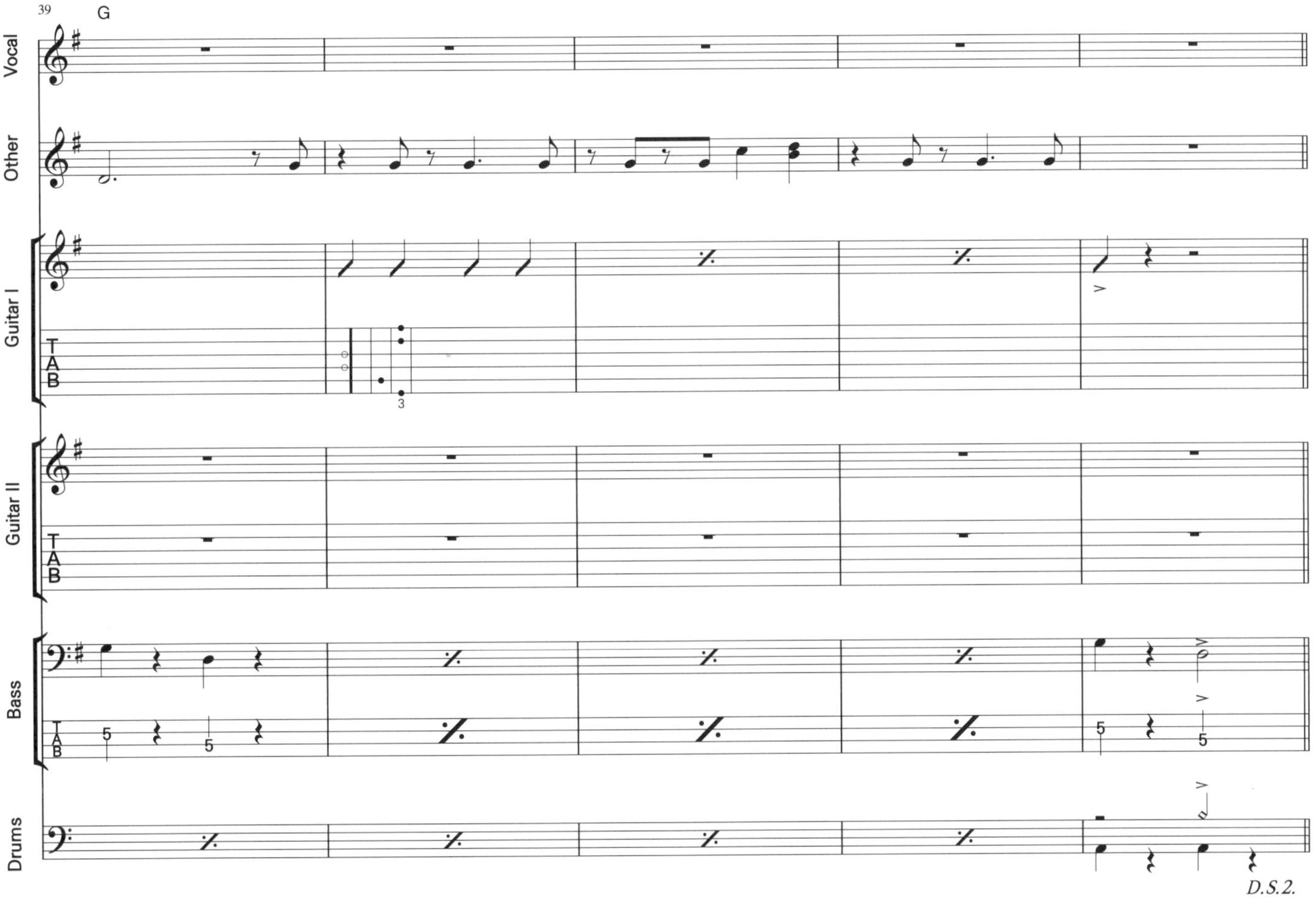
39
G
Vocal
Other
Guitar I
TAB
Guitar II
TAB
Bass
TAB
Drums
D.S.2.

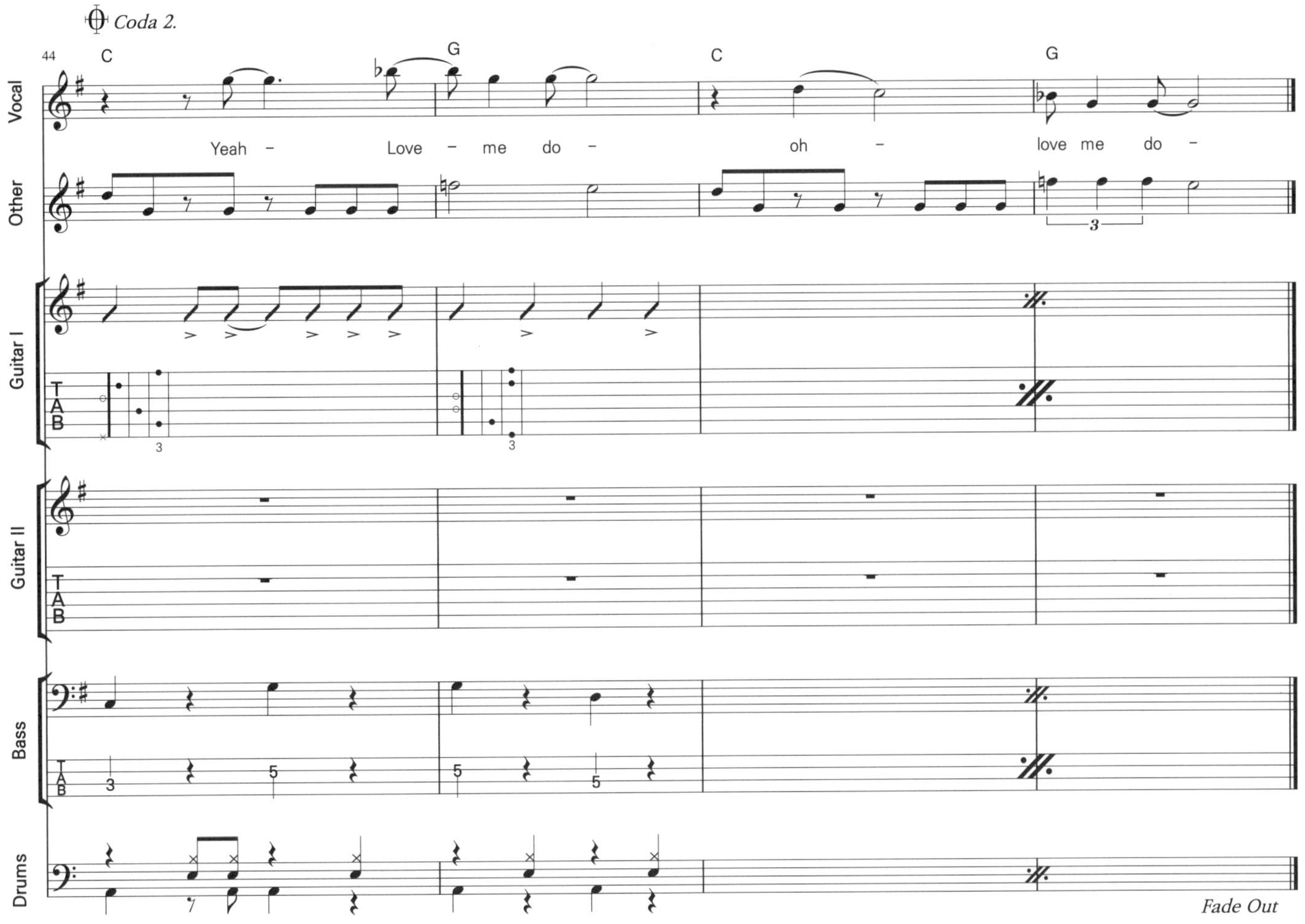
Coda 2.
44
C
G
C
G
Vocal
Yeah – Love – me do – oh – love me do –
Other
Guitar I
TAB
Guitar II
TAB
Bass
TAB
Drums
Fade Out

# Twist And Shout

Words & Music by
Bert Russell, Phil Medley

Well, shake it up ba — by, — now
Twist and
Shake it up ba — by
shout —
Come on, — come on, — come on, — come on, ba — by — now, —
Twist and shout —
Come on ba —

A7   D   G   A7
Vocal
Come on and Work it on out, —   —
1. Well, — work it on out, —
2.3. You know you twist, lit – tle girl, —
Chorus
— by   Work it on out   Woo —
Guitar I
Guitar II
Bass
Drums

C
D   G   A7   D   G   A7
Vocal
— — hon – ey   You know you look so good   You know you got me
You know you twist so fine   Come on and twist a lit – tle
Chorus
1. Work it on out —   Look so good —
2.3. Twist lit – tle girl —   Twist so fine —
Guitar I
Guitar II
Bass
Drums

to ⊕  1.
17  D  G  A7  D  G  A7
go-ing  now —  Just like I knew — you would —  Well, shake it up ba-
clo-ser  now —
Got me  go — ing  Like I knew you  would  Woo —
Twist a lit-tle clo-
Vocal
Chorus
Guitar I
Guitar II
Bass
Drums
2.
21  A7  D  G  A7
And let me know — that you're mine — — —  Woo —
— er  Let me know you're  mine  Woo —

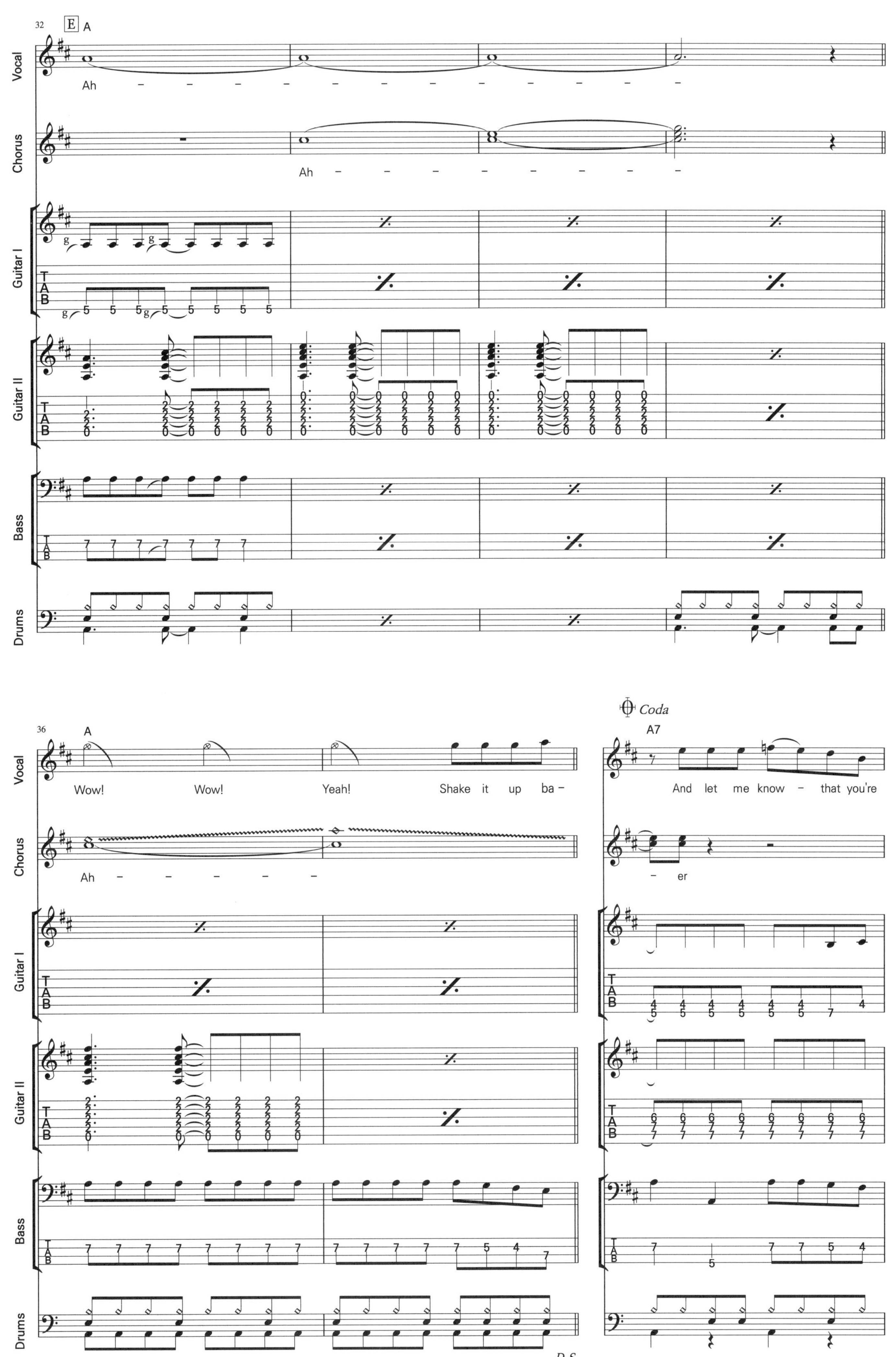

32
E
A
Vocal
Ah
Chorus
Ah
Guitar I
g
Guitar II
Bass
Drums
36
A
Wow!
Wow!
Yeah!
Shake it up ba –
Ah
Guitar I
Guitar II
Bass
Drums
Coda
A7
And let me know – that you're
– er
D.S.

Vocal
Chorus
Guitar I
Guitar II
Bass
Drums
mine
Well, shake it, shake it, shake it, ba - by, - - now -
Let me know you're mine
Woo -
Shake it up, ba -
Well, shake it, shake it, shake it, ba - by, - - now -
Well, shake it, shake it, shake it,
- by
Shake it up, ba - by

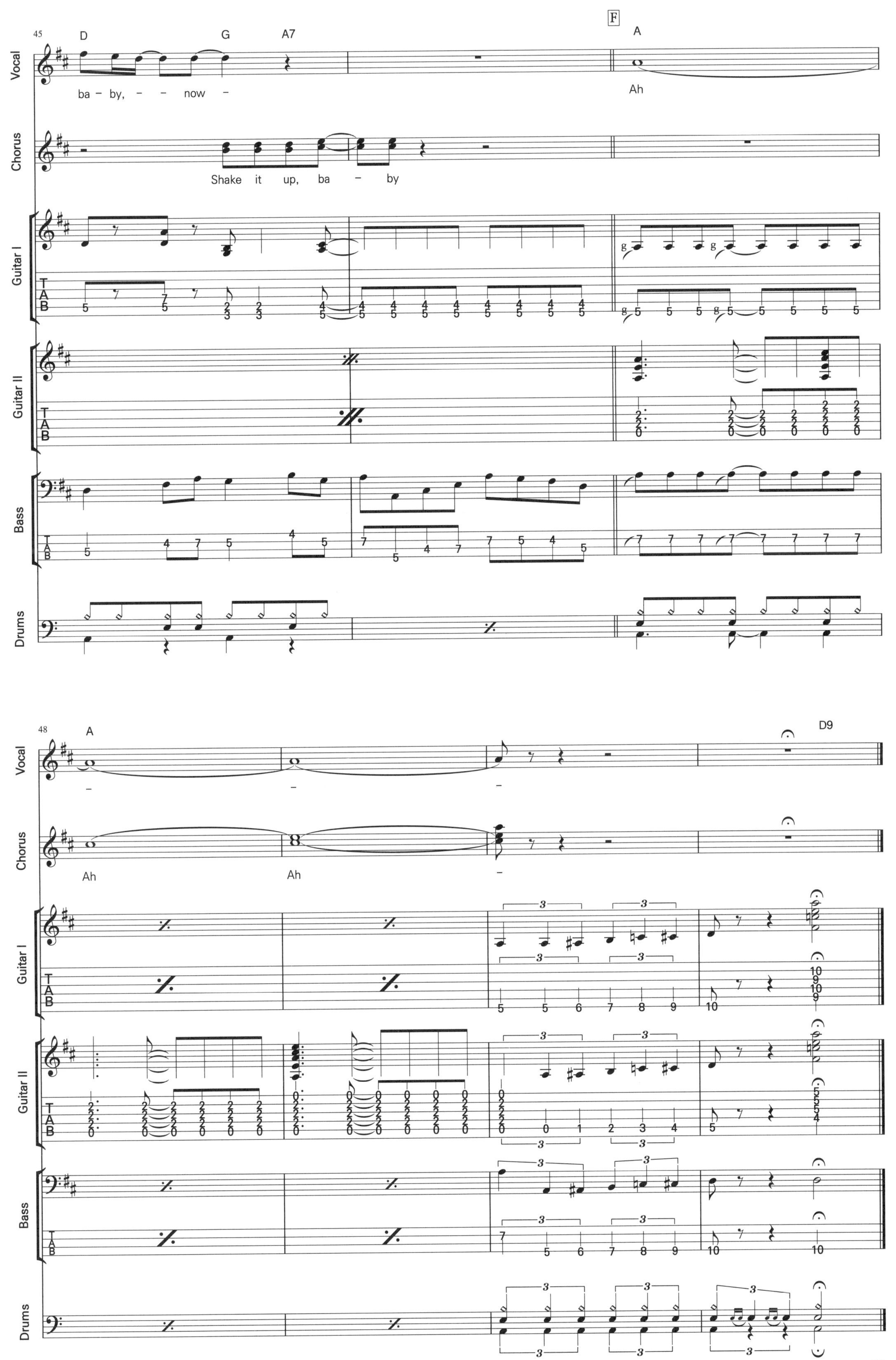

45
D    G    A7    F    A
Vocal
ba - by, - - now -    Ah
Chorus
Shake it up, ba - by
Guitar I
Guitar II
Bass
Drums

48
A    D9
Vocal
-    -    -
Chorus
Ah    Ah    -
Guitar I
Guitar II
Bass
Drums

# It Won't Be Long

Words & Music by
John Lennon, Paul McCartney

long yeah Till I be- long to you
yeah Ah - -
Eve-ry night when eve - ry - bo - dy has fun Here am I
Eve-ry night the tears come down - from my eyes Eve-ry day
eve-ry day we'll be hap - py, I know Now I know that

sit - ting all - on my own
I've done no - thing but cry
you won't leave - me no more

1. 2. It won't be
3. It won't be

long yeah yeah yeah It won't be long - yeah yeah yeah It won't be
long yeah yeah yeah It won't be long - - yeah yeah yeah It won't be

20
C#m
to ⊕ A
A(b9)
E
Vocal
long yeah Till I be-long to you Since you
long yeah Till
Chorus
yeah Ah - -
Guitar I
S
H.C
H.C
S
H.C
Guitar II
Bass
H
H
Drums
24
D
E
D#aug
D6
C#7
Vocal
left me I'm so a-lone - Now you're com-ing. you're com-ing on home -
Chorus
You left me I'm - so a - lone Now you're co - ming on
Guitar I
Guitar II
Bass
Drums
37

I'll be good like I know I should You're com-ing home, - you're com-ing home
home I should com - ing on home - -
I be-long to - you Woo
Ah woo - - -
So
home
Coda
Slow
D.S.

38

# All My Loving

Words & Music by
John Lennon, Paul McCartney

4
Vocal
Chorus
Guitar I
Guitar II
Bass
Drums
C#m
A
F#m
D
- you - Re - mem - ber - I'll al - ways - be true
- ing - And hope - that - my dreams - will - come true
- you - Re - mem - ber - I'll al - ways - be true
8
B7
B F#m
B
E
And then while I'm a - way - I'll write home eve - ry - day -
And then while I'm a - way - I'll write home eve - ry - day -

Vocal
Chorus
Guitar I
Guitar II
Bass
Drums
C#m
A
B
E
And I'll send all my lov – ing – to you –
And I'll send all my lov – ing – to you –
E
E
C#m
C#mM7/C
I'll pre – tend –
All my lov – ing, –
I – will send to you –
Woo –
1.
2.3.
C

20
E
C#m
C#mM7/C
Vocal
Chorus
Guitar I
Guitar II
Bass
Drums
All – my lov–ing, – darl – ing, I'll – be true –
– Woo –
24
E
to
D A
Vocal
Chorus
Guitar I
Guitar II
Bass
Drums
–

28
E
F#m
B7
Vocal
Chorus
Guitar I
TAB
Guitar II
TAB
Bass
TAB
Drums
Coda
32
E
E
Close your eyes –
Close your eyes –
All – my
H
H
3
3
3
3
D.S.

E
C#m
Vocal
lov-ing – All – – – my lov-ing Woo – All – my –
3
Chorus
Woo – Woo –
Guitar I
Guitar II
Bass
Drums

C#m
E
Vocal
3
lov-ing – I will send to you
Chorus
Woo – Woo
Guitar I
Guitar II
Bass
Drums

# From Me To You

A
Vocal
Am
da
C
If there's an-y-thing that you want —
Am
If there's an-y-thing I can do —
C
Other
Guitar I
Guitar II
Bass
Drums
G7
Just call on me —
F
and I'll send it a-long —
Am
with love —
C
from me —
G7
to you
to
Vocal
Other
Guitar I
Guitar II
Bass
Drums

Vocal
Other
Guitar I
Guitar II
Bass
Drums
C
Am
B  C
Vocal 2x tacet
Am
I've got eve-ry-thing that you want, – Like a
2x only
2x only
S
S
S
2x only
S
S
S
S
C
G7
(Vocal 2x tacet)
F
heart – that's oh so true – Just call on me – and I'll
(2x only)
(2x only)
(2x only)

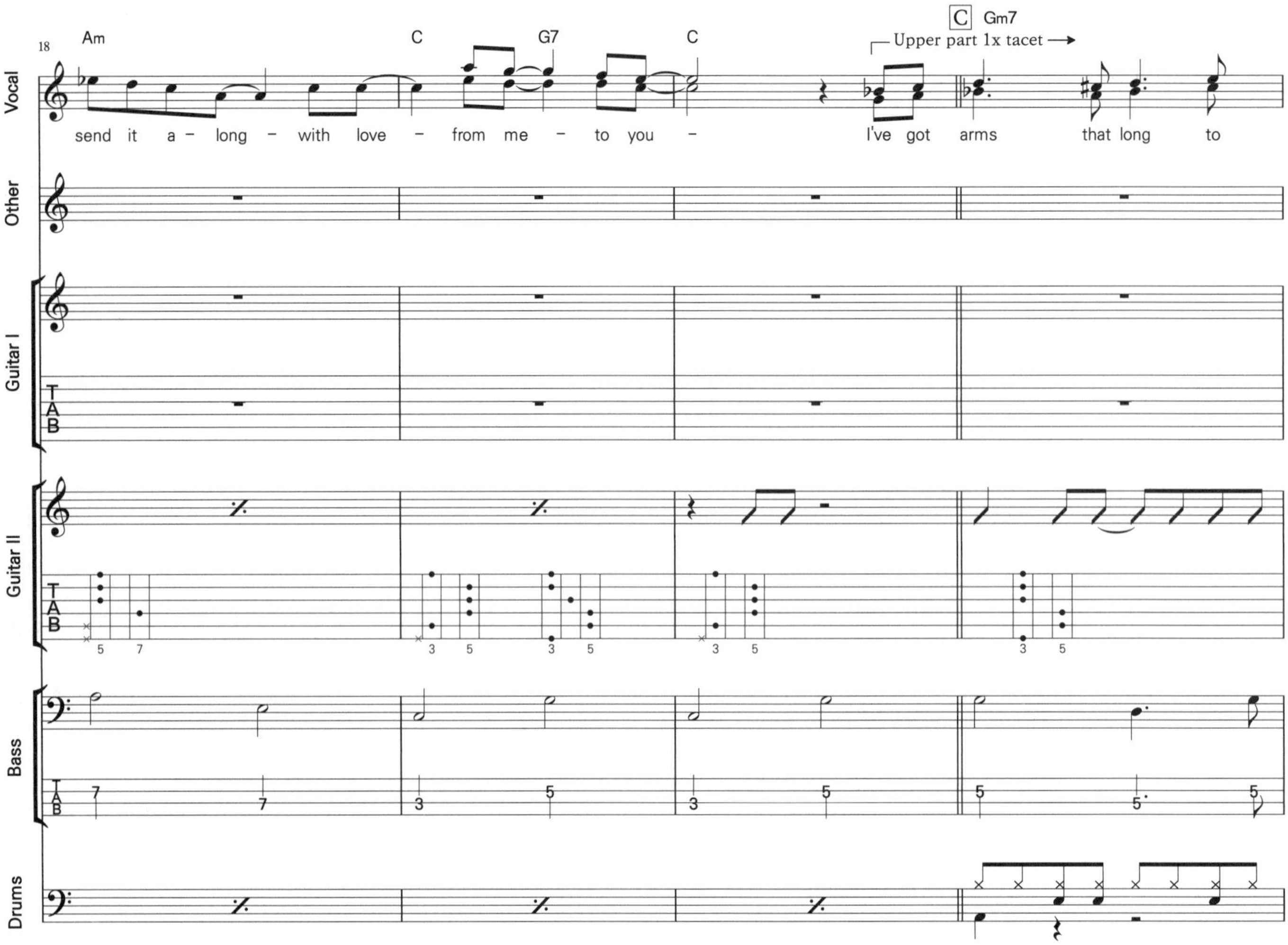

18
Am
C
G7
C
C
Gm7
Upper part 1x tacet
send it a – long – with love – from me – to you – I've got arms that long to
Vocal
Other
Guitar I
Guitar II
Bass
Drums


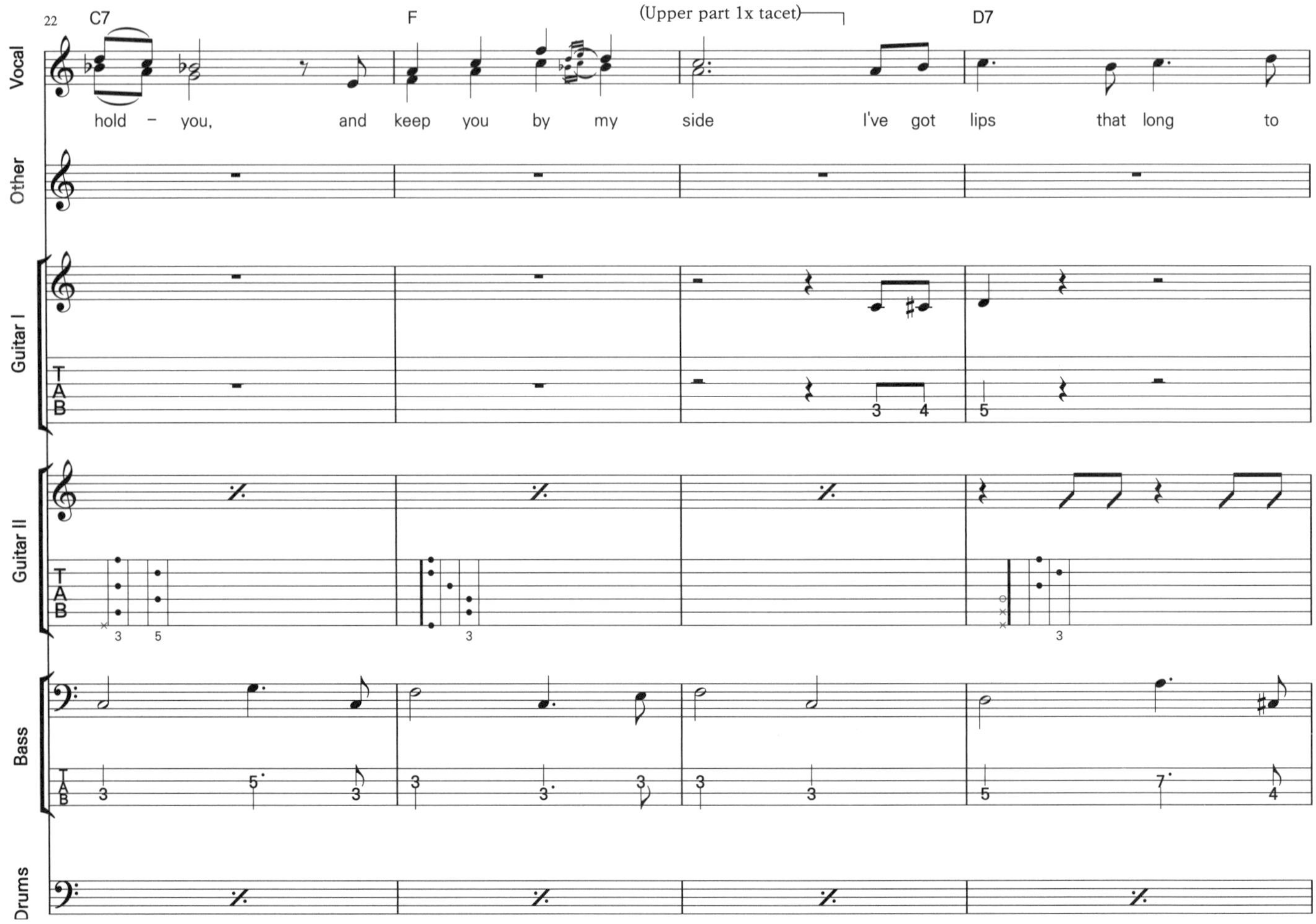

22
C7
F
(Upper part 1x tacet)
D7
hold – you, and keep you by my side I've got lips that long to
Vocal
Other
Guitar I
Guitar II
Bass
Drums

kiss - you, and keep you sat - is - fied. Ooo, If there's - fied. Ooo, If there's
To you - to you - to you

# She Loves You

Words & Music by
John Lennon, Paul McCartney

yeah, yeah, – she loves you, yeah, yeah, yeah, yeah!
(Straight)
1. You think you've lost your love, – Well, I saw her yes - ter -
2. She said you hurt her so, – She al - most lost her
3. You know it's up to you, – I think it's on - ly

12
Vocal
Guitar I
Guitar II
Bass
Drums
D7
G
Em7
Bm
- day - yi - yay.
It's you she's think - ing of, -
And she told me what to
mind, - -
But now she says she knows -
You're not the hurt - ing
fair, - -
Pride can hurt you too, -
A - pol - o - gize to

16
D7
B G
Em
- day - yi - yay. She says she
She says she loves you, and you know that can't be bad.
kind, - -
her, - -
Be - cause she

52

20
Vocal
Guitar I
Guitar II
Bass
Drums
Em
Cm
1.
D7
Yes, she loves you, and you know you should be glad.
24
Vocal
Guitar I
Guitar II
Bass
Drums
D7
2.
D7
C
Em
She  Oo  She loves you, yeah,

28
Vocal
Guitar I
Guitar II
Bass
Drums
Em
A7
Cm
yeah, yeah, – she loves you, yeah yeah, yeah, – And with a love like that you
3
3
32
Vocal
Guitar I
Guitar II
Bass
Drums
D7
to
G
know you should be glad. – – – You
S S
S S
3
3
D.S.

Coda
And with a love like that you know you should be glad.-
And with a love like that you know you should - - -

43
D7
D G
Em6
Vocal
be glad. - Yeah,
Guitar I
Guitar II
Bass
Drums
47
Em6
C
G6
yeah, yeah, - Yeah, yeah, yeah, yeah,

# I Want To Hold Your Hand

Words & Music by
John Lennon, Paul McCartney

Oh yeah, I'll - - tell you some - thing -
I think you'll un - der - stand When I - - say that

some - thing -
I wan - na hold your hand -
I wan - na hold your hand - - - - - -
I wan - na hold your -

hand
1. Oh please – – – say to me – –
2.3. you – – – got that some – thing. –
and let me be your man,
I think you'll un – der – stand.
And please – – say to
When I – – say that
D.S.x (feel)
60

me - - You'll let me hold your hand, - Now, let me hold your
some - thing. - I wan - na hold your hand, - I wan - na hold your
hand - - - - - - I wan - na hold your - hand,
hand - - - - - - I wan - na hold your - hand, And when I
U D
C
G
Em
to
C
D7
G
C Dm7
Upper Part 1x tacet

touch you, I feel hap-py in-side -- It's such a feel-ing that my
love I can't hide -- I can't hide, -- I can't hide --
(Upper Part 1x tacet)

Vocal
Guitar I
Guitar II
Bass
Drums
39
1.
2.
Coda
D
D7
C
D7
Yeah,
Yeah,
I wan - na hold your
C D C C D C C C D
D.S.
42
B7
C
D7
C
G
hand
I wan - na hold your hand
63

# Can't Buy Me Love

Words & Music by
John Lennon, Paul McCartney

Can't buy me love
I'll
1. buy you a dia - mond ring -
2. give you all I've got -
3.4. you don't need no -
my friend -
to give -
dia - mond rings -
if it makes you feel al - right -
if you say you love me too -
And I'll ve sa - tis - fied -
I'll
Tell -
H.H.Open
D.S.time

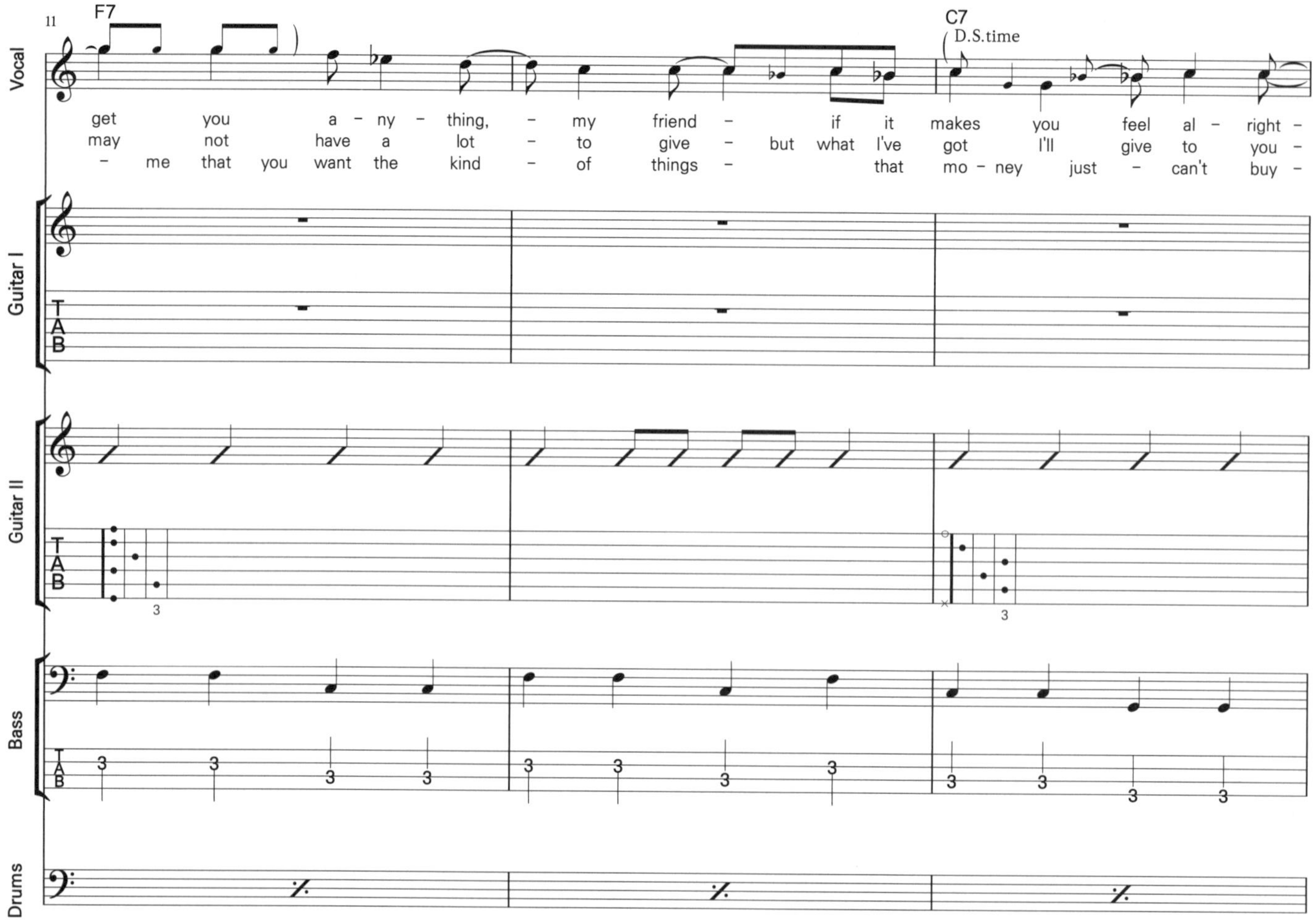
11
F7
C7
D.S.time
Vocal
get you a – ny – thing, – my friend – if it makes you feel al – right –
may not have a lot – to give – but what I've got I'll give to you –
– me that you want the kind – of things – that mo – ney just – can't buy –
Guitar I
Guitar II
Bass
Drums

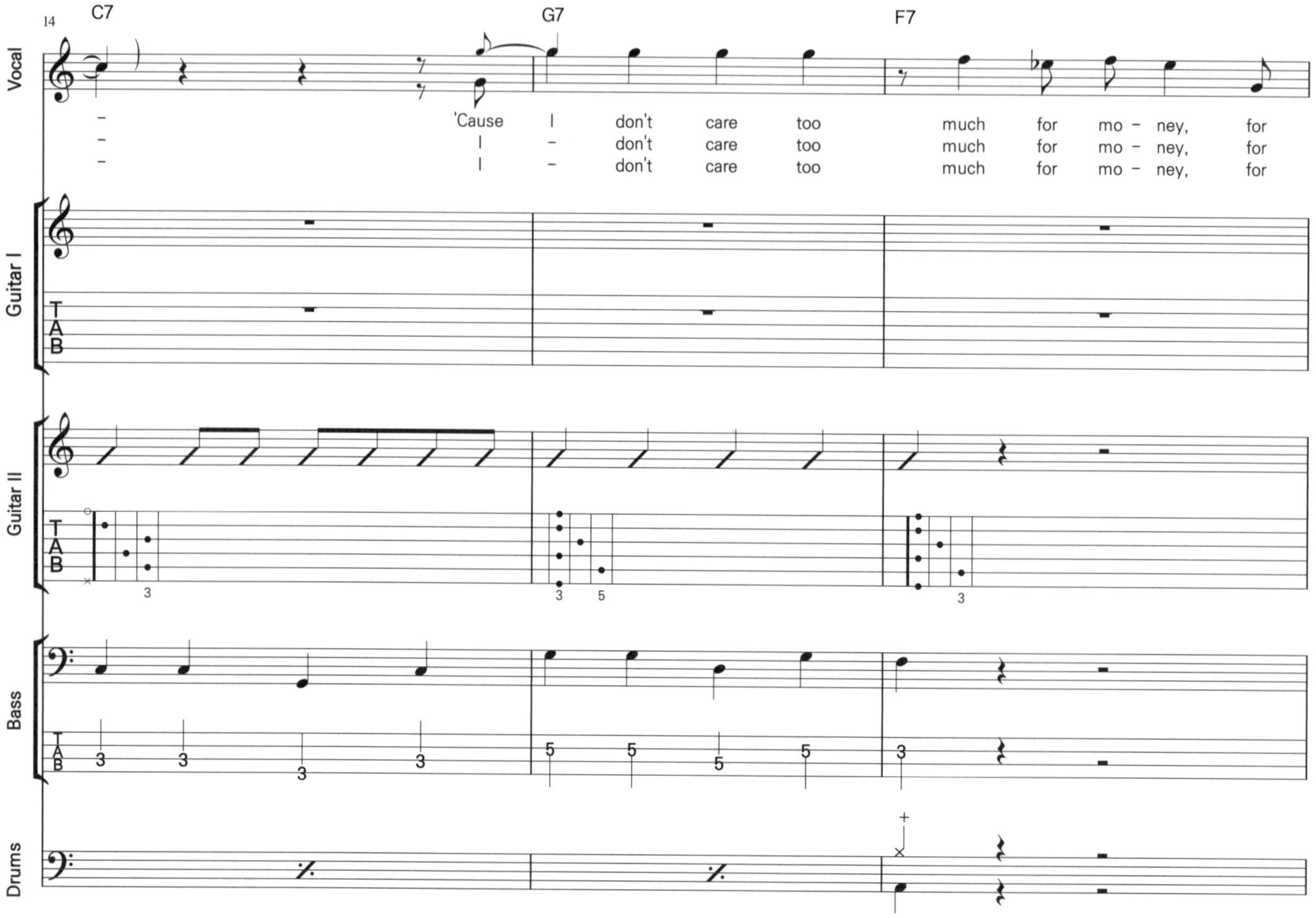
14
C7
G7
F7
Vocal
– 'Cause I don't care too much for mo – ney, for
– I – don't care too much for mo – ney, for
– I – don't care too much for mo – ney, for
Guitar I
Guitar II
Bass
Drums

17
F7
Vocal
mo - ney can't buy me love -
mo - ney can't buy me love -
mo - ney can't buy me love -
to 1.2. C7
I'll - Can't buy me love, -
1.
2.
C7
Guitar I
Guitar II
D.S.2 time
3
3
Bass
3 3 3 3
3 3 3 3
3 3 3 3
D.S.2 time
H.H.Open
Drums

20 C Em
Vocal
- - -
eve - ry - bo - dy tells me so -
Am
C7
Guitar I
3
3
Guitar II
3
3
3
Bass
7 7 7 7
5 5 5 5
3 3 3 1
Drums

23
C7
Em
Am
Vocal
Guitar I
Guitar II
Bass
Drums
— Can't buy me love, —   —   —
Coda 1.
26
Dm7
G6
C7
No,   no,   no,  —   no!   Say —
—   Ah —
D.S. 1.

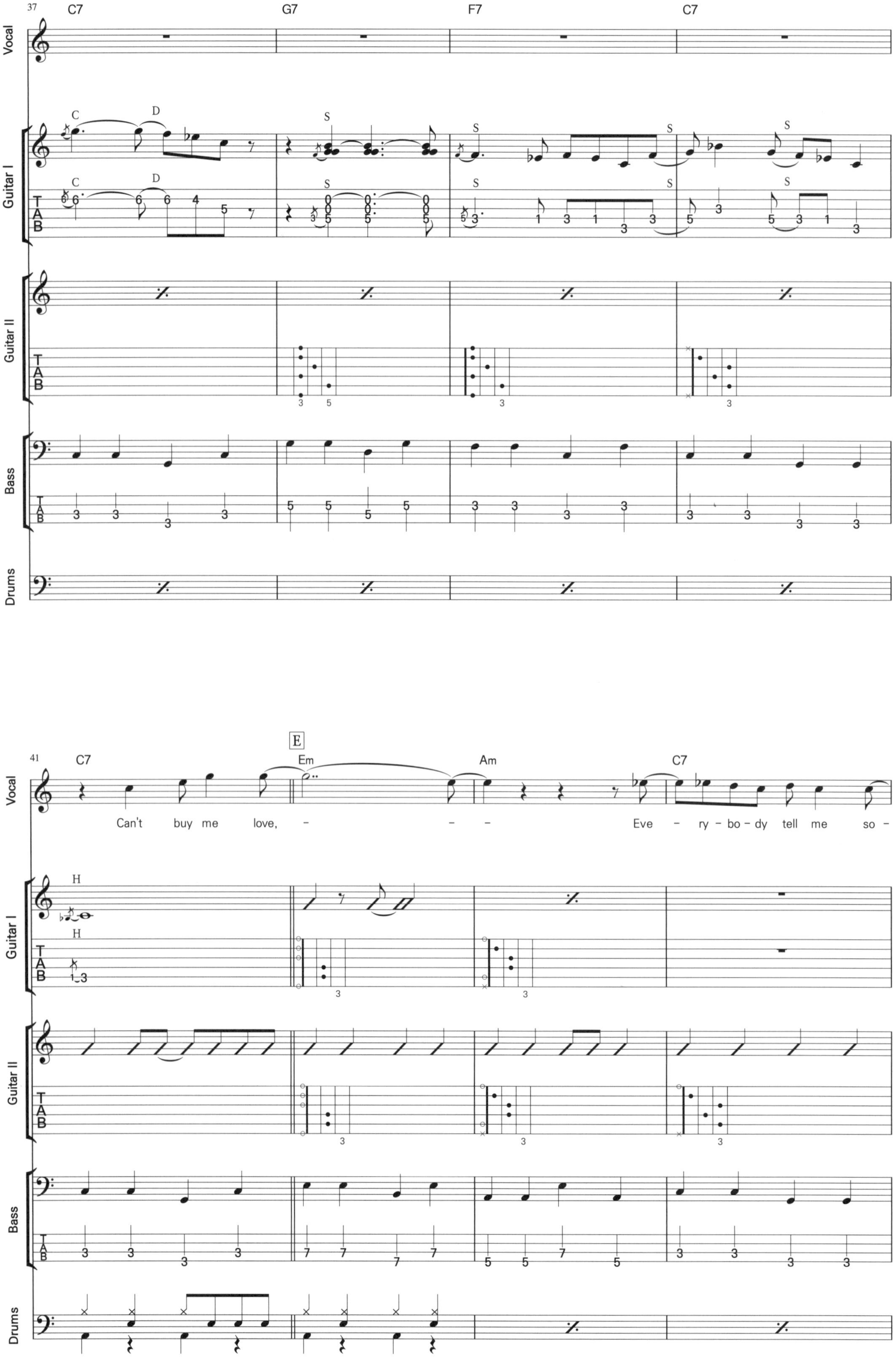

Can't buy me love, — — — — Eve – ry – bo – dy tell me so –

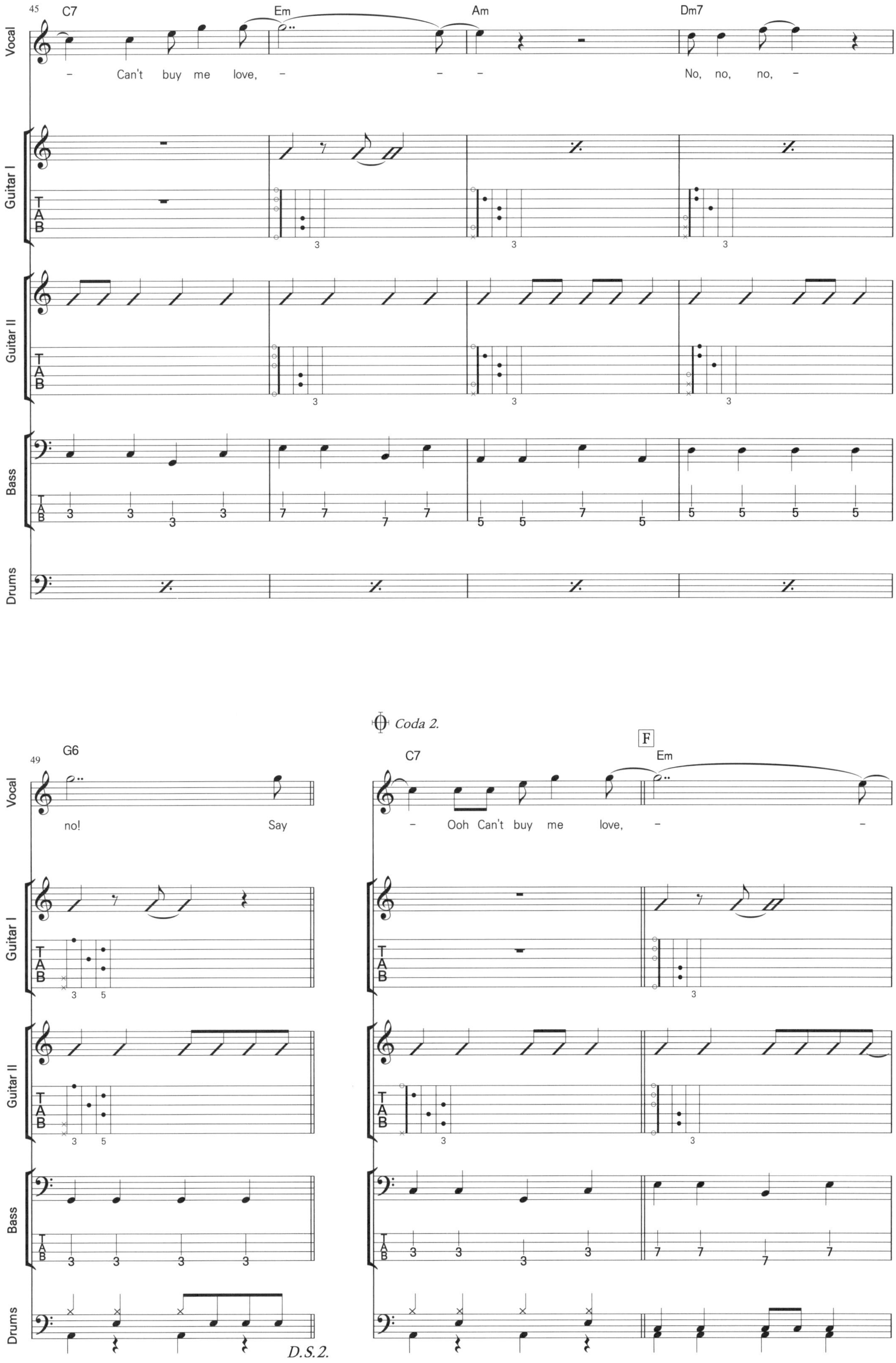

45
C7    Em    Am    Dm7
Vocal
Guitar I
Guitar II
Bass
Drums
– Can't buy me love, –    –    –    No, no, no, –
Coda 2.
49
G6    C7    F    Em
no!    Say    – Ooh Can't buy me love, –    –
D.S.2.

52
Vocal
Guitar I
Guitar II
Bass
Drums
Am
Em
Am
love
Can't buy me love
55
Dm7
G6
C7
mu
72

# A Hard Day's Night

Words & Music by
John Lennon, Paul McCartney

work-ing — like a dog — It's been a hard day's night —
mo-ney — to buy you things — And it's worth it just to hear you say —
I should be sleep-ing — like a log — But when I
You're gon-na give me — eve-ry-thing — So why on

74

(Straight)
1. get home to you I find the things that you do will make me feel — al — right —
2.3. earth should I moan 'Cause when I get you a — lone You know I feel — O. — K. —
You know I — When I'm home —

eve - ry - things seems - to be right - when I'm home -
feel - ing you hold - ing me tight tight -

Yeah – It's been a hard day's night – and I've been work-ing – like a dog –
It's been a hard day's night – I should be sleep-ing – like a log –
D.S.x ( like a

But when I get home to you I find the things that you do will make me feel — al — right —
log — )
Oh! —

So why on

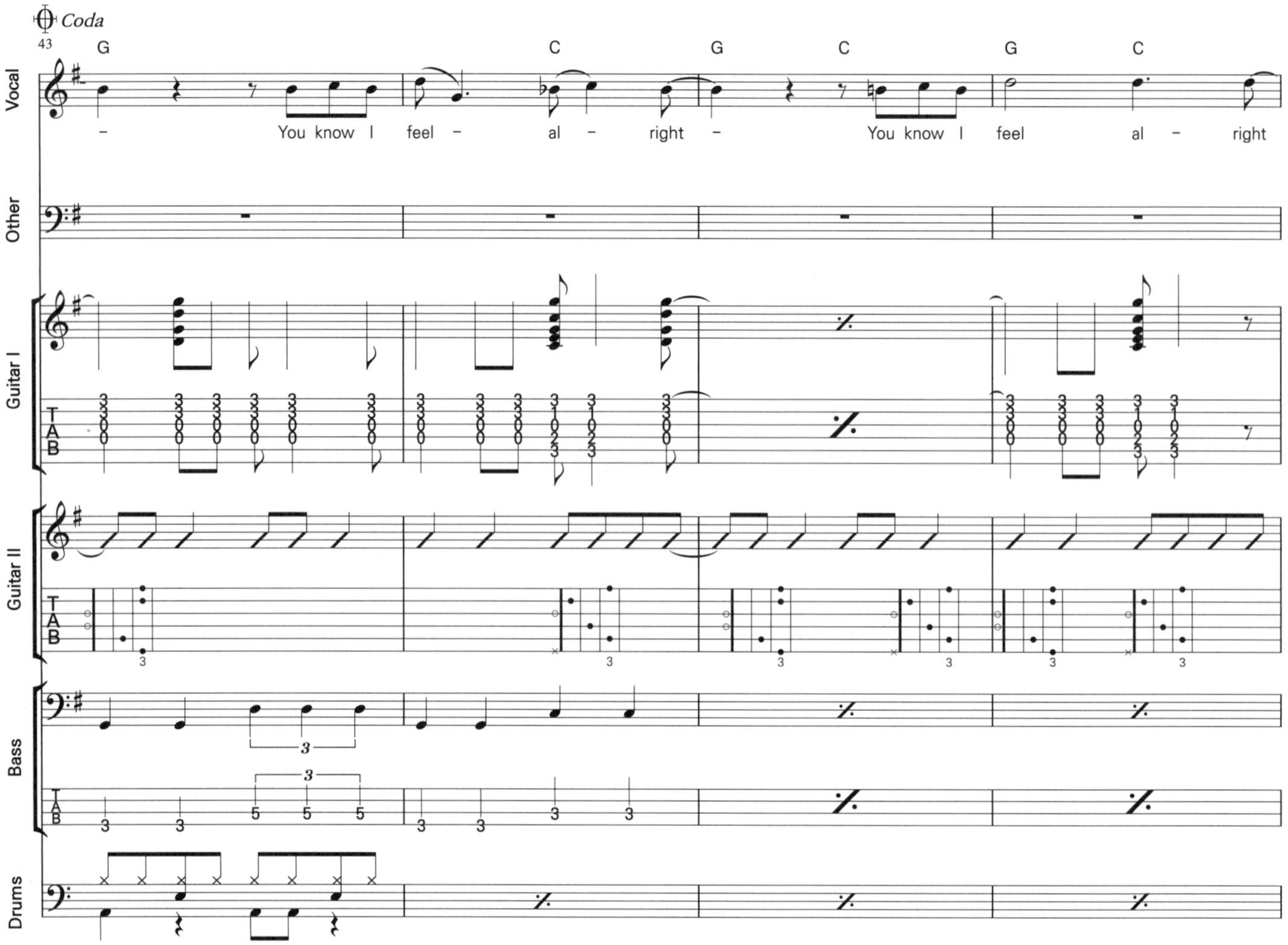

Coda
43
G          C          G          C          G          C
Vocal
Other
Guitar I
Guitar II
Bass
Drums
- You know I feel - al - right - You know I feel al - right
47
F(add9)/D     F/D     F(add9)/D     F/D     F(add9)/D     F/D     F(add9)/D     F/D
Arpeggio
Arpeggio
(Arpeggio)
(Arpeggio)
Repeat & F.O.

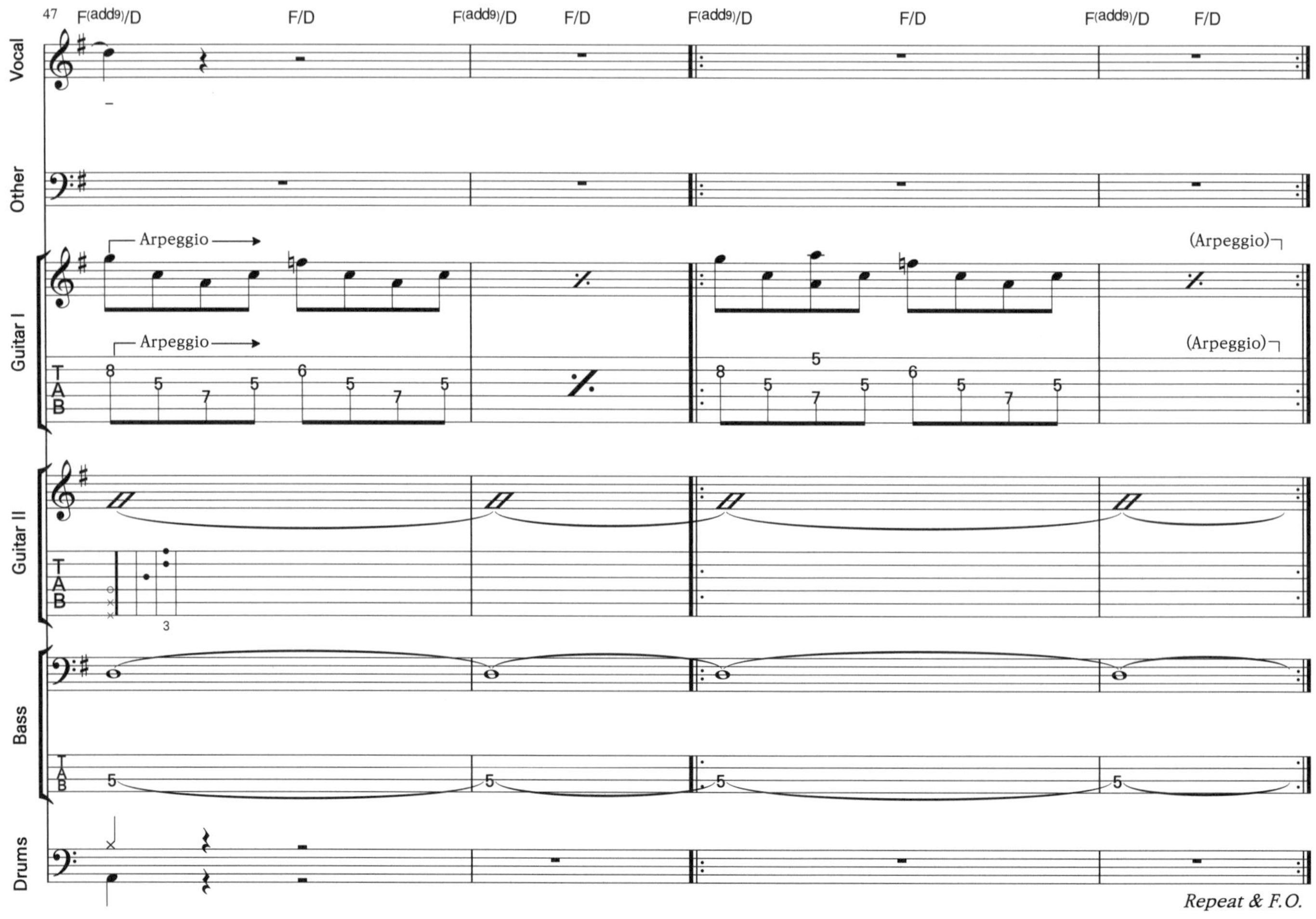

# And I Love Her

Words & Music by
John Lennon, Paul McCartney

Vocal
Guitar I
Guitar II
Bass
Perc.
F#m
C#m
F#m
C#m
1. I give her all — my love — that's all I do — — —
2. She gives me eve-ry - thing — and ten-der - ly — — —
3. Bright are the stars — that shine, — dark is the sky — — —
1x tacet →
1x tacet →
F#m
C#m
A
B7
And if you saw — my love — you'd love her too — I — love—
The kiss my lov - er brings — she brings to me — And I love—
I know this love of mine — will ne - ver die — And I love—
82

her
her
her
A love like ours
could ne - ver die
As long as I have you

near me

30
C  F  D  Gm  Dm
Bright are the stars – that shine, –
35
Gm  Dm  Gm  Dm  Bb
dark is the sky – – – I know this love of mine – Will ne-ver die-
Vocal
Guitar I
Guitar II
Bass
Perc.

40
C7
F6
E
Gm
And I love – her –
Ooh –
45
F6
Gm
D
86

# Rock And Roll Music

Words & Music by
**Chuck Berry**

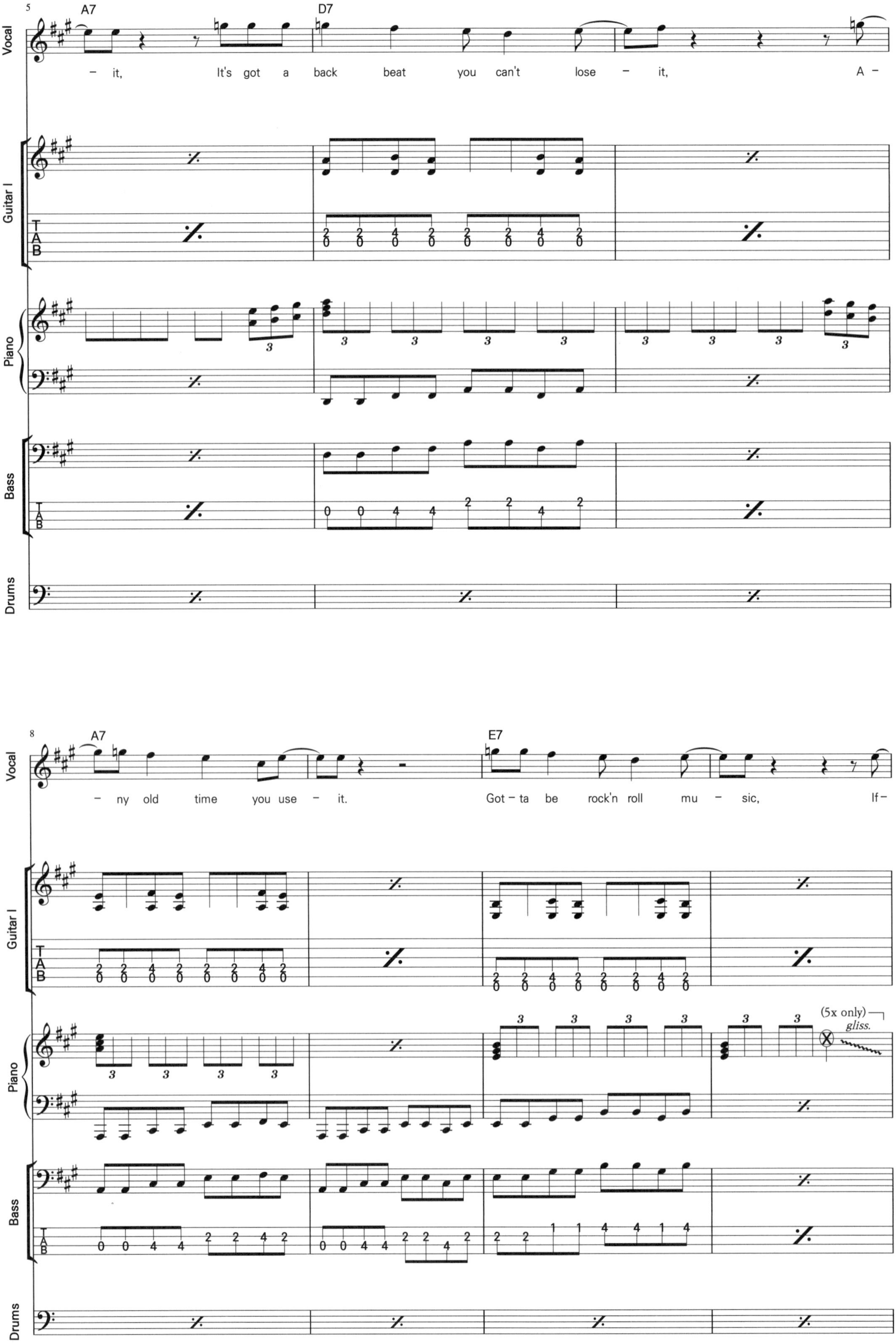
5
A7
D7
Vocal
– it, It's got a back beat you can't lose – it, A –
Guitar I
TAB
Piano
Bass
TAB
Drums
8
A7
E7
– ny old time you use – it. Got – ta be rock'n roll mu – sic, If –
(5x only)
gliss.

1.2.3.4.
12
Vocal
E7   A7   E7   A7
- you wan - na dance with me - if - you wan - na dance with me I've got no kick a - gain - st
I took my loved one o - ver
Way down - south they had a
Don't care to hear 'em play a
Guitar I
Piano
Bass
Drums
gliss.
B
16
Vocal
E7   A7
mod - ern jazz, - Un - less they try to play it too darn fast -
across the tracks, - So she can hear my man a wail a sax -
ju - bi - lee, - The joke - y folks thay had a jam - bo - ree -
tan - go, - I'm in the mood to hear a man - bo -
Guitar I
Piano
Bass
Drums

A7
D7
Vocal
And lose the beau — ty of the me — lo — dy, —
I must ad — mit thay have a rock — in' band, —
They're drink — in' home — brew from a wa — ter cup, —
It's way too ear — ly for a con — go, —
Un — til thay sound just like a
Man, tha were go — ing like a
The folks — danc — in' got —
So keep a — rock — in' that pi —
Guitar I
Piano
Bass
Drums
E7
A7
5.
sym — pho — ny —
hur — ri — cane —
all shook up —
— a — no —
That's why I go for that
That's why I go for that
And start — ed play — in' that
That's why I go for that
Repeat 5 times

# Eight Days A Week

Words & Music by
John Lennon, Paul McCartney

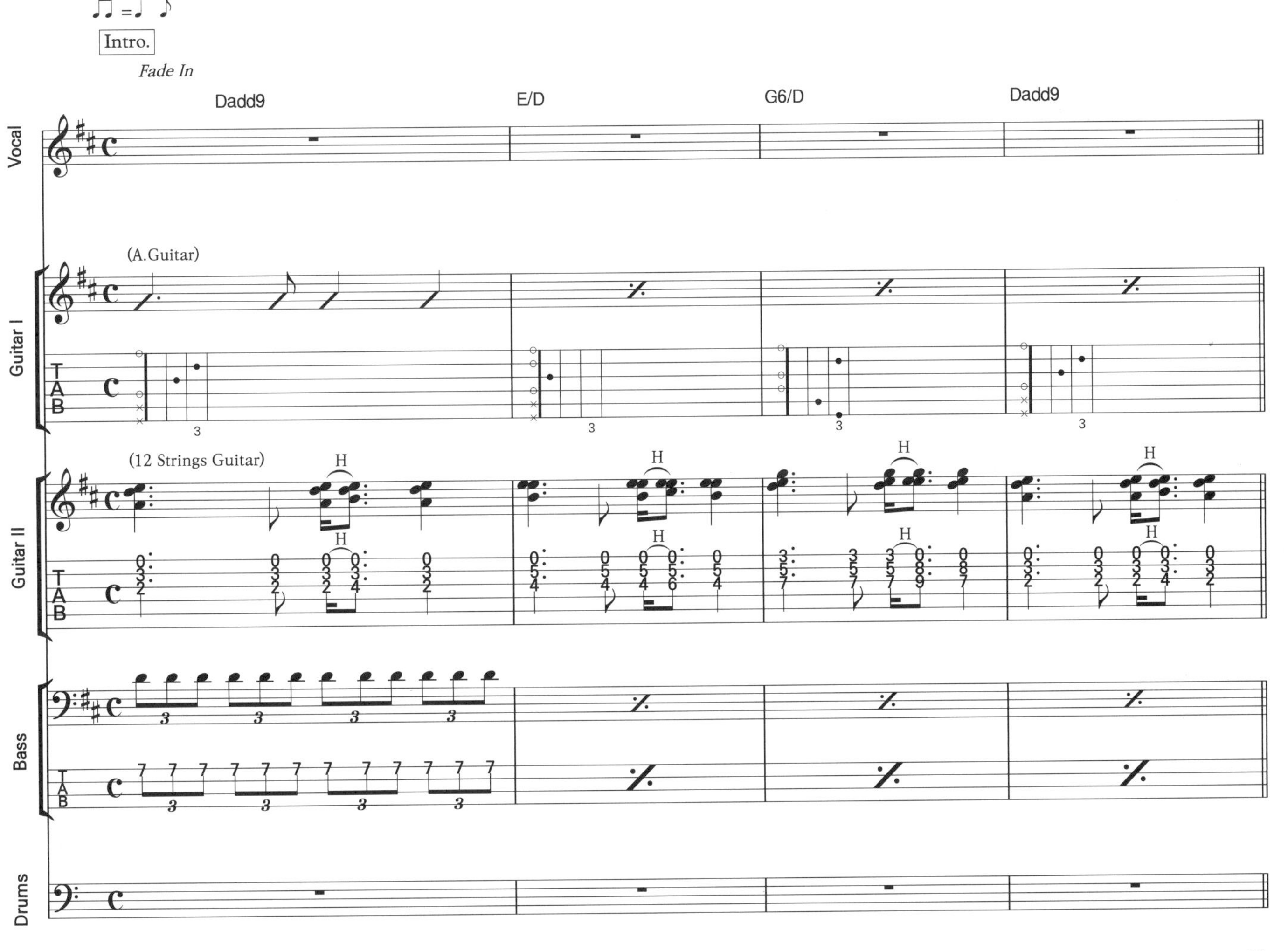

A 1.2. (Straight)
Vocal
Guitar I
Guitar II
Bass
Drums
D    E    G    D
1.3. Ooh, I need your love, babe, – guess you know it's true –
2.4. Love you eve – ry day, girl, – al – ways on my mind –
3
(H.Clap)
D    E    G    D
B
Bm
2,4x with Chorus
Hope you need my love babe, – just like I need you – Hold me, –
One thing I can say girl, – love you all the time –
4
3
(H.Clap)

love me, – hold me, – love me – I ain't got no-thing but love, babe, –
2.4. (girl, –)
Eight days a week – – – Eight days a week I
(2,4x with Chorus)
to 2.

23
Bm
E
Vocal
Guitar I
Guitar II
Bass
Drums
love - - - - you
Eight days a week is
27
G
to Coda 1.
A
Coda 1.
A
not e - nough to show I care -
show I care -
D.S.1.
D.S.2.
94

Coda 2.
Vocal
Guitar I
Guitar II
Bass
Drums
G
D
G
D
Eight day's a week, – – –
eight day's a week – – –
D
Dadd9
E/D
G6/D
Dadd9
H
H
H
H
H
H

# I Feel Fine

Words & Music by
John Lennon, Paul McCartney

6
G7
G
Vocal
Chorus
Guitar I
TAB
Guitar II
TAB
Bass
TAB
S
S
Drums
(Rim Shot)
A (Straight)
10
G7
Vocal
1. Ba - by's good to me - you know, She's hap - py as - can be, - you know, - She said -
2.3. Ba - by's says she's mine, - you know, - She tells - me all - the time, - you know, - She said -
Chorus
Guitar I
TAB
Guitar II
TAB
Bass
TAB
Drums
97

D7
C7
Vocal
Chorus
Guitar I
Guitar II
Bass
Drums
— so
— so
I'm in love with her — and I feel —
I'm in love with her — and I feel —
G7
G7
fine.
fine.
fine.
fine.

B
22
G    Bm    C    D7    G
Vocal
I'm    so    glad    that she's my lit-tle girl - - -    She's so
Chorus
I'm    so    glad    Ooo    -    She's so
Guitar I
Guitar II
Bass
Drums

27
Bm    Am    D7    G7
Vocal
glad    she's tell-ing all - the world -    That her ba - by buys her things -
Chorus
glad    Ooo    -
Guitar I
Guitar II
Bass
C
Drums

31
G7
D7
Vocal
Chorus
Guitar I
Guitar II
Bass
Drums
- you know - He buys her dia - mond rings - you know, - she said - so.
35
D7
C7
to G7
She's in love with me - and I - feel - fine Mm -
She's in love with me - and I - feel - fine
H H
H H

48
C7
G7
Vocal
Chorus
Guitar I
Guitar II
Bass
Drums
Coda
52
G7
G7
fine.
fine.
D.S.
102

She's in love with me – and I – feel – fine
She's in love with me – and I – feel – fine
Mm –
Mm –
Repeat & F.O.
103

# Help!

Words & Music by
John Lennon, Paul McCartney

E7
A7
Vocal
Chorus
Guitar I
Guitar II
Bass
Drums
Perc.
You know I need some - one,
Help!
Help!
B
A
C#m
When I - was young - er, so - much young - er than - to - day,
And now my life has changed - in, oh, so ma - ny ways,
When, - when I - was young I ne - ver
Now - my life has changed My in - de -

13
F#m
D
G
A
Vocal
I ne–ver need–ed an–y–bo–dy's help in an–y way. –
My in–de–pen–dence seems to va–nish in the haze. –
Chorus
need – help in an–y way. –
pendence – va–nish in the haze. –
Guitar I
Guitar II
3
3
3
3
Bass
4. 4 4
5. 5 5
7. 7 7 5
Drums
Perc.

17
C A
C#m
Vocal
1.3. But now these days are gone, – I'm not so self–as–sured, – –
2. But eve–ry now and then – I feel so in–se–cure, – –
Chorus
1.3. Now – these days are gone And now – I
2. But – – now and then I know – I
Guitar I
Guitar II
3
5
Bass
7. 7 7
4. 4 6
Drums
D.S.time no H.H.
(Tambourine)
D.S.time only

Now I find I've changed my mind, I've op-ened up the doors.
I know that I just need you like - I've ne-ver done - be-fore.
find I've op-ened up the doors.
that I've ne-ver done - be-fore.
(no H.H)
(D.S.time only)
Help me if you can, - I'm fell-ing down, - - And I do-

29
G
Vocal
- ap - pre - ci - ate - you be - ing 'round - -
Chorus
Guitar I
Guitar II
3 5
Bass
3 3 5 5
3 3 2 2
Drums
Perc.
33
E7
Vocal
Help me get - my feet - back on the ground. - - Won't you
Chorus
Help me get - my feet - back on the ground. - - Won't you
Guitar I
Guitar II
3
Bass
0 0 4 4 2 2 4 2
Drums
Perc.

please
please help me?
please
please help me?
When I was younger, so much younger than today,
(Top center)

I ne-ver need-ed an-y-bo-dy's help in an-y way
me? me, me! Oo
me? Help Help me! Oo
Coda
D.S.

# You've Got To Hide Your Love Away

Words & Music by
John Lennon, Paul McCartney

It she's gone I can't go on -- Feel-ing two foot small --
Hear-ing them -- see-ing them -- In the state I'm in --
Eve-ry-where peo-ple stare -- each and -eve-ry day - I can see them laugh at me --
How could she say to me -- "Love will find a -way" Gath-er round -- all you clowns --
(1x tacet)

Vocal
Guitar I
Guitar II
Perc. Drums
C    F    C    D    D/C    D/B    D/A    C    G    C
And    I - hear them say
Let    me - hear you say
Hey    you've got to hide    your - love a-
Arpeggio
Arpeggio
(Shaker)
Dsus4    D    Dadd9    D    G    C    Dsus4 D Dadd9 D
- way
Hey    you've got to hide your - love a - way
TAB

D
15
G   D   FM7   G   C   FM7   C
(Flute)
Vocal
Guitar I
Guitar II
Drums
Perc.
17
G   D   F   G   C   F   C   G
Vocal
Guitar I
Guitar II
Drums
Perc.

# Ticket To Ride

Words & Music by
John Lennon, Paul McCartney

1.2. (Straight)
A
Vocal
1.3. think I'm gon - na be sad — — I think it's to - day — Yeah! —
2.4. said that liv - ing with me — — is bring - ing her down — Yeah! —
Other
Guitar I
Guitar II
Bass
Drums
A
— The Girl that's driv - ing me mad — — is go - ing a - way
— For she would ne - ver be free — — when I was a - round

D.S.1. ( Yeah – oh! ) She's got a tic – ket to ride –
D.S.2. ( oh! )
She's got a tic – ket to ride – – – –

Vocal
Other
Guitar I
Guitar II
Bass
Drums
17
F#m
E
A
to 2.
She's got a tic-ket to ride- but she don't care - - - -
20
1.
A
2.
A
B
D7
She
I don't know why she's rid-ing so high-
118

She ought to think twice she ought to do right by me Be-
fore she gets to say-ing good-bye
She ought to think twice she ought to do right by

Coda 1.
to 1.
Coda 2.
D.S.1.
D.S.2.
me
I
She
My ba-by don't - care
My ba-by don't -
Hand Clap
120

35
A
Vocal
care
My ba – by don't – care
Other
Guitar I
TAB
Guitar II
H.C D   C D   H.C D   C D   H.C D   H.C D   C D   H.C
Bass
Drums
38
A
Vocal
My ba – by don't – care
My ba – by don t – care
Other
Guitar I
TAB
Guitar II
H.C C   H.C   H.C   H.C   H.C   H.C D   C D   H.C
Bass
Drums
Fade Out

# Yesterday

Words & Music by
John Lennon, Paul McCartney

(Straight)
1. Yes - ter-day - all my trou-bles seemed so
2. Sud - den-ly - I'm not half the man - I
3.4. Yes - ter-day - love was such an ea - sy
[ Tuning : Whole Step Down ]
( A.Guitar )
( Strings )
D.S.2x
( Cello )
1x tacet
1x tacet

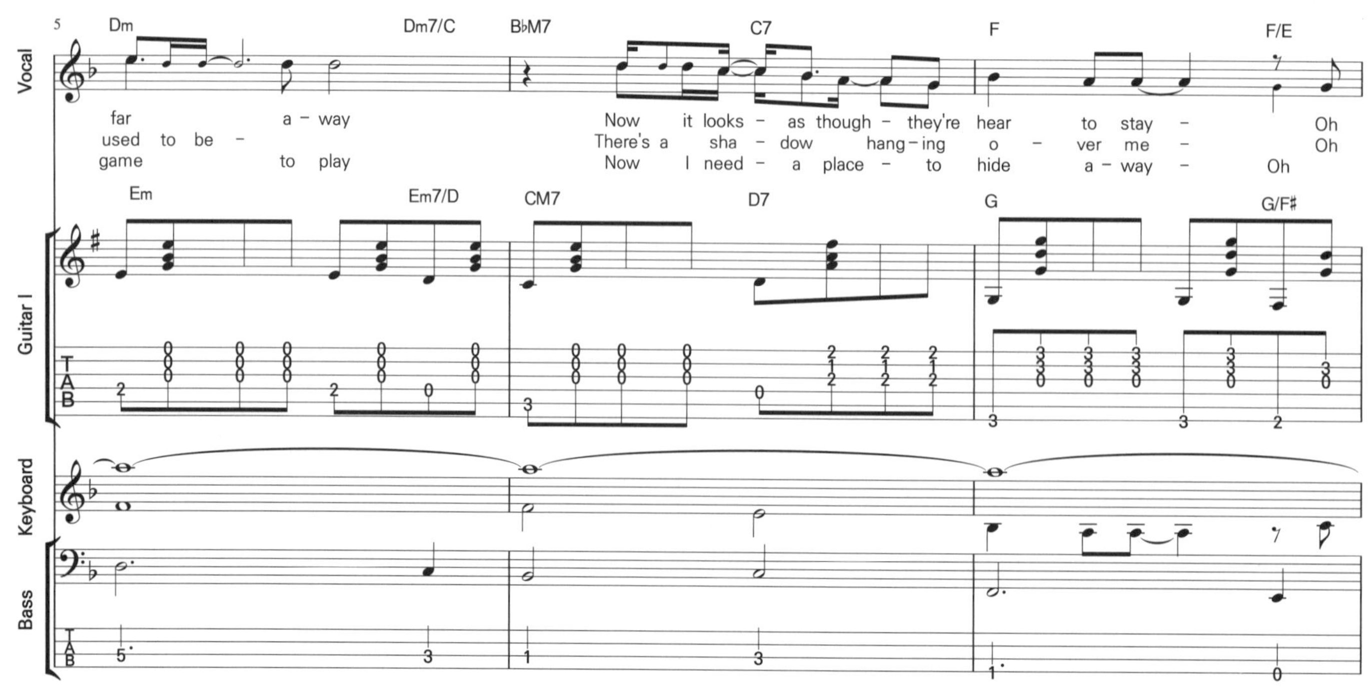

far a - way
used to be - to play
game to play
Now it looks - as though - they're hear to stay - Oh
There's a sha - dow hang-ing o - ver me - Oh
Now I need - a place - to hide a - way - Oh

to Coda 2. B
I believe in yesterday
Why she had to go I don't know she wouldn't say
yesterday came suddenly
I believe in yesterday
I said something wrong now I long for yesterday
Coda 1.
Coda 2.
day
day
Mm
D.S.1.
D.S.2.

# Drive My Car

Words & Music by
John Lennon, Paul McCartney

wan - ted to be
pros - pects were good
start right a - way
She said "Ba - by can't you see?
And she said "Ba - by it's un - der - stood
And she said "Listen babe, I've got some-thing to say
I wan-na be fa-mous a star of the screen
Work - ing for pea - nuts is a - ll very fine
I got no car and it's break - ing my heart
But you can do some - thing
But I can show you a
But I found a dri - ver and

in be - tween"
be - tter time"
that's a start"
"Ba - by, you can drive my car -
yes, I'm gon -na be a star -
Ba - by, you can drive my car -
And may -be I'll love-

Beep beep mm beep beep, yeah
(Tambourine)
127

"Ba- by, you can drive my      car -

yes, I'm go - nna be a star -
Ba - by, you can drive my car -
And may - be I'll love - you"
D.S.
129

Coda
D    G    E
Vocal
- you"
Beep beep mm beep beep,   yeah -
Other
Guitar I
8va,1x tacet →
1x tacet →
Guitar II
S
S
Bass
Drums
Perc.
G
Vocal
Beep beep mm   beep beep      yeah, -
Beep beep mm beep beep,    yeah -
Other
(8va bassa)
Guitar I
(8va,1x tacet)
(1x tacet)
Guitar II
Bass
Drums
Perc.
Repeat & F.O.

# Norwegian Wood (This Bird Has Flown)

Words & Music by
John Lennon, Paul McCartney

I once – had a girl – Or should I say she once had me She showed – me her room Is– n't it
good Nor –we–gian wood? She asked me to stay And she told me to sit a– ny where – So
told me she worked in the morn –ing And start –ed to laugh –
1x only

I looked a-round And I no-ticed there was-n't a chair —
told her I did-n't And crawled off to sleep in the bath —
I sat on a rug bi-ding my
And when I a-woke I was a-

time Drink-ing her wine.
-lone This bird has flown
We talked un-til two And then she said "It's time for bed —"
So I lit a fire Is-n't it

17
D E
Vocal
Other
D
Guitar I
D
Guitar II
Bass
Drums
She
2.
E
E E
Vocal
good Nor-we-gian wood?
Other
D
Guitar I
H
H
D
Guitar II
Bass
Drums
134

# Nowhere Man

Words & Music by
**John Lennon, Paul McCartney**

Vocal
Other
Guitar I
Guitar II
Bass
Drums
F#m
Am
to E
Ma - king all - his no - where plans for no - bo - dy
Ma - king all - his no - where plans for no - bo - dy
Em
Gm
D
B
E
B
A
E
1.3. Does - n't have - a point of - view - Knows not where he's go - ing to -
2. He's as blind as he can be - Just sees what he wants to see -
1.3. Does - n't have - a point of - view - Knows not where he's go - ing to -
2. He's as blind as he can be - Just sees what he wants to see -
1x only
1x only
D
A
G
D

Is-n't he a bit like you and me? No-where man,
No-where man, can you see me at all? No-where man,
Is-n't he a bit like you and me?
No-where man, can you see me at all?
please li-sten You don't know what-you're miss-ing No-where man
don't wo-rry Take your time, don't hur-ry Leave it all
Ah Ah la la la Ah Ah la la la

the world – – – is at your com – mand
till some – bo – dy else lends you a hand
Ah Ah la la la Ah Ah la la la la la
1x tacet
1x tacet
138

Vocal
Other
Guitar I
Guitar II
Bass
Drums
29
F#m
Am
E
Harm.
Harm.
S S
S S
Em
Gm
D
2.
3.
Coda
B7
B7
E
Ah
la la la la
Ah
la la la la
no - bo -dy
no - bo -dy
A7
A7
D
D.C.

Vocal
Other
Guitar I
Guitar II
Bass
Drums
36
E
F#m
Am
E
Ma - king all - his no - where plans for no - bo - dy
D
Em
Gm
D
40
E
F#m
Am
E
Ma - king all - his no - where plans for no - bo - dy -
Ma - king all - his no - where plans - for no - bo - dy
D
Em
Gm
D

# Michelle

Words & Music by
John Lennon, Paul McCartney

A
F
B♭m7
E♭6
Ddim
C
G7(♭9)
C
Vocal
Other
Guitar I
Guitar II
Bass
Drums
Mi - chelle    ma belle    These are words that
Woo    Woo    Woo
go to - geth - er well    My Mi - chelle -
Woo    Woo    Woo    Woo
(Rim Shot)

Mi - chelle ma belle Sont des mots qui vont trés bien en -
Woo
Woo
Woo
Woo
- semble Trés bien en - semble
Woo
Woo
Woo
1. love you, I love you, I
2. need to, I need to, I
3. want you, I want you, I
3x only
3x only

Vocal
Other
Guitar I
Guitar II
Bass
Drums
Fm
Ab7
Db
C7
Fm
FmM7
love you
need — — — to
want — — — you
That's all I — want yo say
I need to — make you see
I think you — know by now
Woo
Woo
Un — til I find a way — — I will say the on — ly
Oh, what you mean to me — — Un — til I do, I'm
I'll get to you some — how — — Un — til I do, I'm
Woo Woo Woo Woo Woo Woo

24
Fm7    Fm6    B♭m/F    to    1. C    2. C
Vocal
words  I  know  That  you'll  un - der - stand
hop - ing  you  will  know  what  I  mean
tell - ing  you  So  you'll  un - der -
Other
Guitar I
Guitar II
Bass
Drums

D
28  F    B♭m7    E♭    Ddim
Vocal
I  love - you
Other
Woo    Woo    Woo    Woo
(E.Guitar)
Guitar I
Guitar II
Bass
Drums

Vocal
Other
Guitar I
Guitar II
Bass
Drums
32
C
Bdim
C
Coda
C
Woo
Woo
Woo
- stand
D.S.
E
35
F
Bbm7
Eb6
Mi - chelle
ma
belle
Sont
des
mots
qui
Woo
Woo
Woo

146

Ddim
C
Bdim
C
F Fm
FmM7
vont tres bien en – semble Tres bien en – semble
And I will say the on – ly words –
Woo Woo Woo Woo
(A.Guitar)
Fm7
Fm6
Bbm/F
C
– I know That you'll un – der – stand My Mi –
Woo Woo

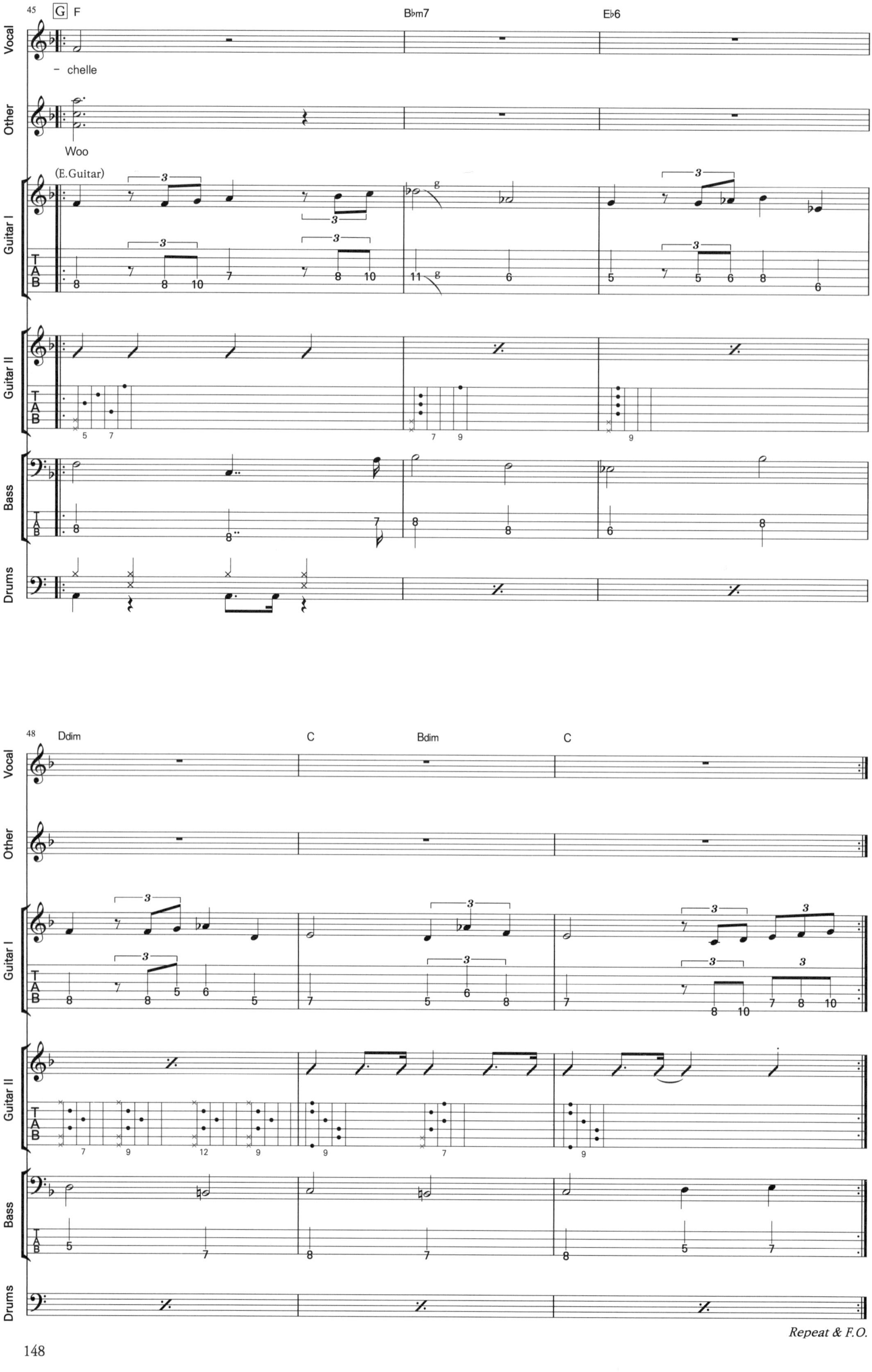
45
G
F
B♭m7
E♭6
Vocal
- chelle
Other
Woo
(E.Guitar)
Guitar I
Guitar II
Bass
Drums
48
Ddim
C
Bdim
C
Repeat & F.O.

# Girl

Words & Music by
John Lennon, Paul McCartney

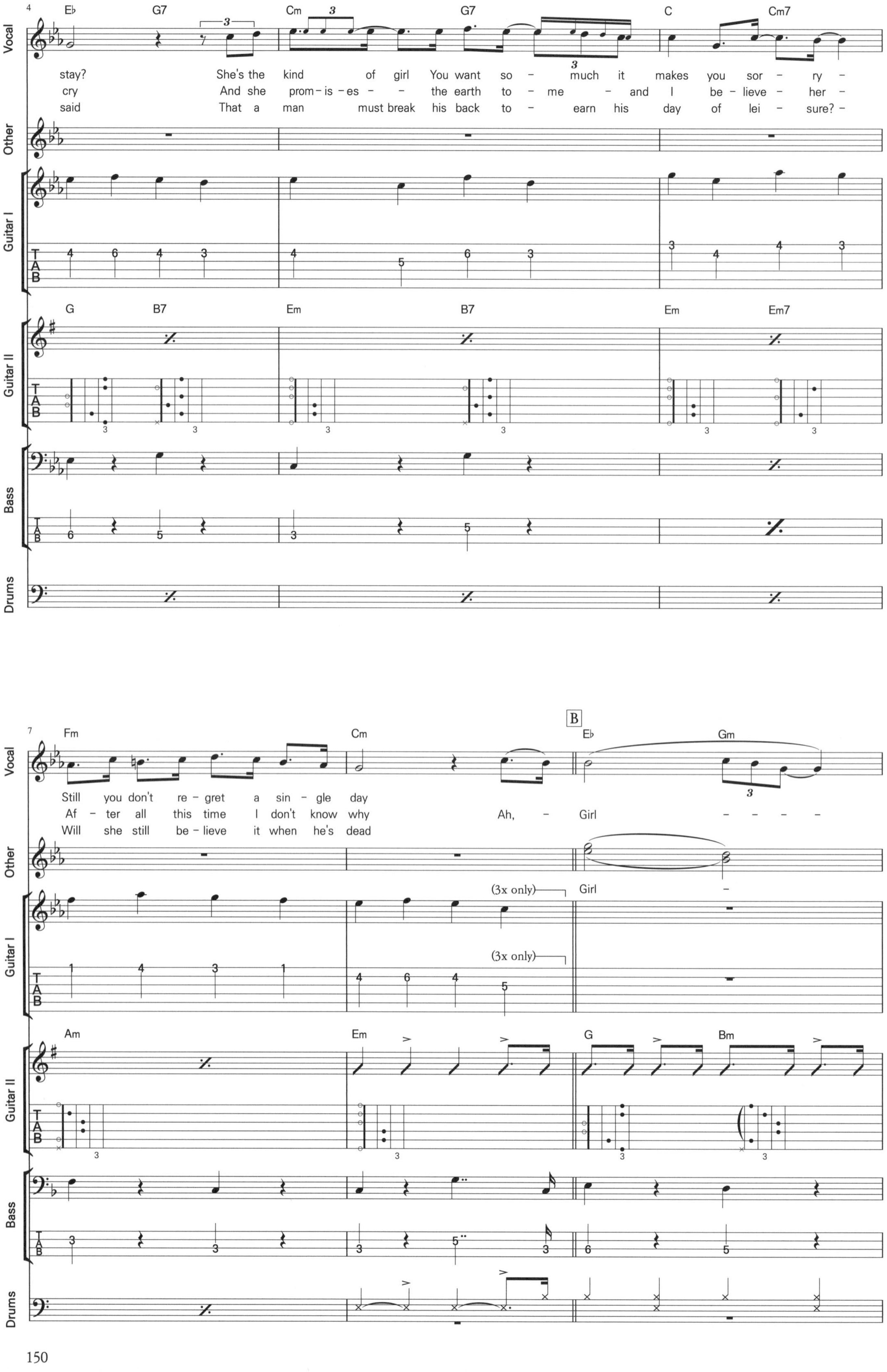

stay? She's the kind of girl You want so — much it makes you sor — ry —
cry And she prom-is-es — — the earth to — me — and I be — lieve — her —
said That a man must break his back to — earn his day of lei — sure? —
Still you don't re — gret a sin — gle day
Af — ter all this time I don't know why
Will she still be — lieve it when he's dead
Ah, — Girl — — —
(3x only) Girl —
(3x only)

Vocal
Other
Guitar I
Guitar II
Bass
Drums
oothss
Girl
Girl
When I
Girl
Girl
tit
She's the kind of girl who puts you down When friends are there You feel a fool

When you say she's look-ing good - She acts as if it's un-der-stood she's
Cool, - ooh, - ...ooo ...ooo ...ooo Girl - - - -
Girl -

Coda
D.S.
153

30
Vocal
Other
Guitar I
Guitar II
Bass
Drums
Eb    G7    Cm    G7    Cm7    Fm
G    B7    Em    B7    Em7    Am
34
Cm    Eb    Gm    Fm    Bb7
Girl
Girl
oothss
Em    G    Bm    Am    D7
Repeat & F.O.
154

# In My Life

Words & Music by
John Lennon, Paul McCartney

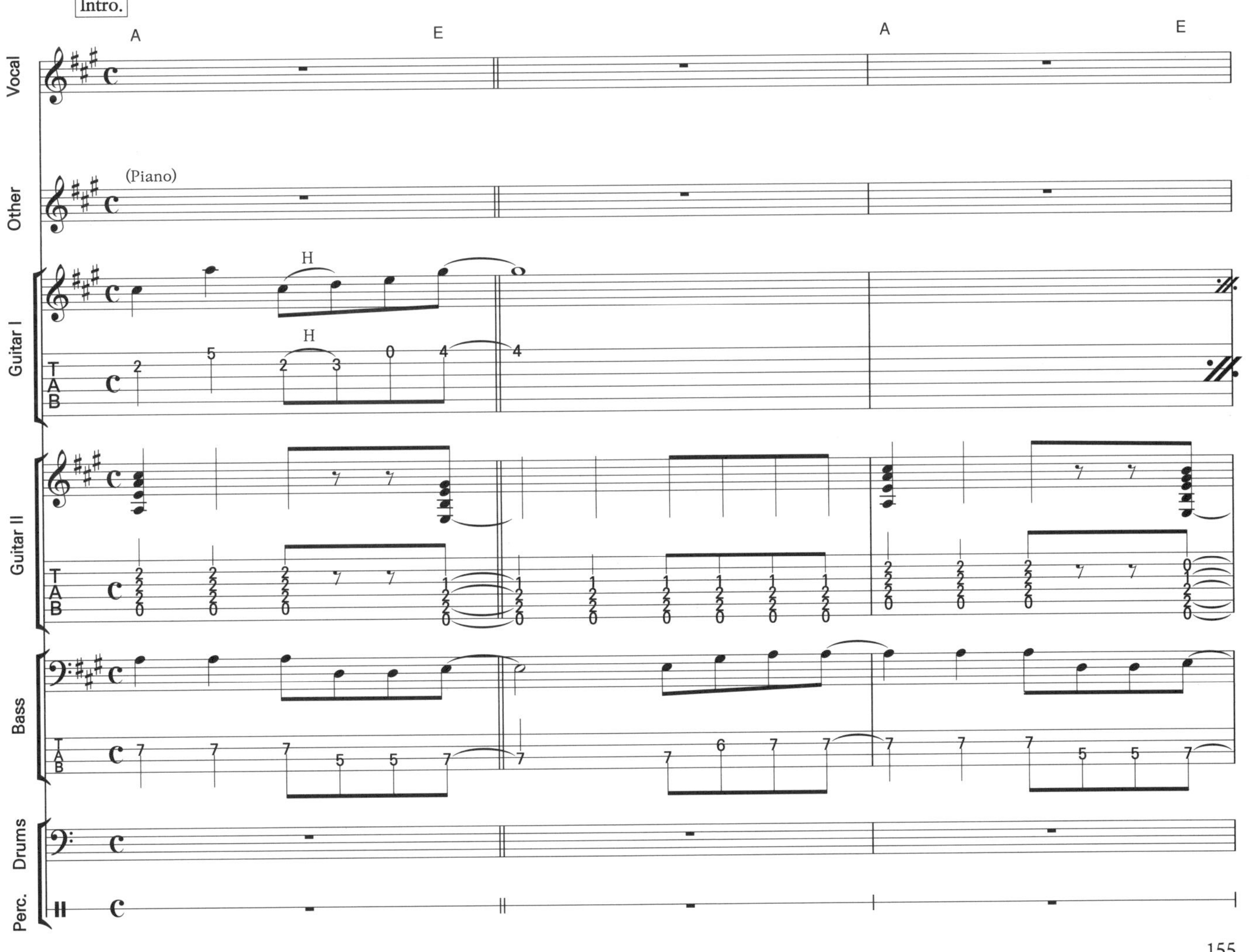

There are pla - ces I'll re - mem - ber all my
all these friends and lo - vers there is

life, - - - though some have changed. - Some for - e - ver, not for
no - - one com - pares with you. - And these memo - ries lose for their

Vocal
Other
Guitar I
Guitar II
Bass
Drums
Perc.
F#m
A7/G
D
Woo
Dm
Woo
A
Woo
be - tter
mean - ing
Some have
when I
gone
think
- of love
and some
as some - thing
re - main.
new.
All these
Though I
B
F#m
D
G
1. pla - ces - had - their - mo - ments
2.3. know - I'll - ne - ver lose af - fec - tion
with lo - vers and - friends -
for peo - ple and - things -
I
that
(Tambourine)

still can re-call — Some are dead and some are liv-ing,
went be-fore, — I know I'll of-ten stop and think a-bout them, In
In
my life I've loved them all. —
my life I

22
Vocal
Other
Guitar I
TAB
Guitar II
TAB
Bass
TAB
Drums
Perc.
E
2. A
C A
E
But of love you more.
8va bassa
8va bassa
3
25
F#m
A7/G
D
Dm
A
Vocal
Other
Guitar I
TAB
Guitar II
TAB
Bass
TAB
Drums
Perc.
3
3
3
3
159

28
A          E          F#m          A7/G          D          Dm
Vocal
Other
Guitar I
T A B
Guitar II
T A B
Bass
T A B
Drums
Perc.
31
A
Vocal
Though I
Other
(8va bassa)
Guitar I
(8va bassa)
T A B
Guitar II
T A B
Bass
T A B
Drums
Perc.
D.S.
Coda
A
D
A          E
love you     more. –
H
H
160

In my life I love you
more.
a tempo
Vocal
Other
Guitar I
Guitar II
Bass
Drums
Perc.
E
Dm7
N.C.
A
E
A
161

# Wait

Words & Music by
John Lennon, Paul McCartney

Vocal
Guitar I
Guitar II
Bass
Drums
Perc.
F#m7   F#m6   Bm/F#   F#m   C#7   F#m   B  A6
D.S.2.x
- way   now -   Oh, how -   I've been a - lone   Wait   till I
heart's   strong -   Hold   on, -   I won't de - lay
(Tambourine)
A6   C#7   to 2.   1.  F#m
come   back - to your   side -   We'll for - get   the   tears we've cried -   But if your
1x tacet
1x tacet

2.3
12
Vocal
Guitar I
Guitar II
Bass
Drums
Perc.
F#m
C
B
E
I feel as though    you ought to know    That I've been
15
A
F#m
B
good,    as good as    I can be    And if you    do,    I'll trust in

164

18
Vocal
you
And know that you
will wait for me
It's been a
Guitar I
Guitar II
Bass
Drums
Perc.
to Coda 1.
E
A
C#7
D.S.1.
Coda 1.
21
C#7
me
But if your
Vocal
Guitar I
Guitar II
Bass
Drums
Perc.
D.S.2.
Coda 2.
F#m
It's been a
long
time
D
F#m7
F#m6

Now I'm – com – ing back home I've been a – way now –
Oh, how – I've been a – lone –

# We Can Work It Out

Words & Music by
John Lennon, Paul McCartney

While you see it your way, - Run a risk of know - ing that our love may soon be gone -
We can work it out. - We can work it out. - -
Think of what you're say - ing, -
Try to see it my way, -

You can get it wrong – and still you think that it's – al – right
On – ly time will tell – if I am right or I – am – wrong
Think of what I'm say – ing –
While you see it your way –
We can work it out and get it straight, or say good night – –
There's a chance that we might fall a – part be – fore too long – –
We can work it out –

Vocal
Guitar
Keyboard
Bass
Drums
16
G
A7
C
Bm
We can work it out. — — Life is ver - y short, — and there's no time —
T A B
G
F#
Bm
Bm/A
19
— — — — — — for fuss — ing and fight — ing, my friend.

22
Bm/G    Bm/F#    Bm
Vocal
Guitar
TAB
Keyboard
Bass
Drums
I    have    al – ways    thought –    that it's a    crime, –

25
G                    F#            Bm            Bm/A
Vocal
Guitar
TAB
Keyboard
Bass
Drums
– – – – – –    So    I    will    ask    you    once    a –

Coda
We can work it out, -
We can work it out. - -

# Day Tripper

Words & Music by
John Lennon, Paul McCartney

5
E7
Vocal
Guitar I
D7
Guitar II
Bass
(Tambourine)
Drums
3
3
3
3
8
E7
Vocal
Guitar I
D7
Guitar II
Bass
(with Tambourine)
Drums
6
6
174

Got a good rea – son for tak – ing the ea – sy way out. –
She's a big tea – ser She took me half – the way there. –
Tried – to please – her She on – ly played – one night stands. –

Got a good rea – son for
She's a big tea – ser,
Tried – to please – her,

tak – ing the ea – sy way out – now. She was a Day
She took me half – the way there – now. She was a Day
She on – ly played – one night stands, – now. She was a Day
Trip – per,
Trip – per,
Trip – per,
One way tic – ket, yeah. –
One way tic – ket, yeah. –
Sun – day driv – er yeah. –
It took me

A7
G#7
C#7
to
Vocal
so - - - - long to find out, - and I - found
Guitar I
G7
F#7
B7
Guitar II
S
S
Bass
Drums
1.
B7
E7
Vocal
out.
Guitar I
A7
D7
Guitar II
Bass
(Tambourine)
6
6
Drums

29
E7
Vocal
Guitar I
D7
A7
Guitar II
Bass
Drums
2.
B7
out.
3
3
3
3
3
7 7 6 9 9 6 7
32
C
B7
Vocal
Guitar I
H
H
H
0 1 4 4 2 2 4 2 2 2 4
4
2
A7
Guitar II
(Gt.3)
(Gt.3 Capo : 0f Key = E)
(Gt.3)
3 7 9 6 3 7
Bass
7 7 7 7
Drums

Vocal
Guitar I
Guitar II
Bass
Drums
36
B7
Ah
H.U D
C
A7
39
B7
Ah
Ah
Ah
C
D
H.U
C
U D
A7
179

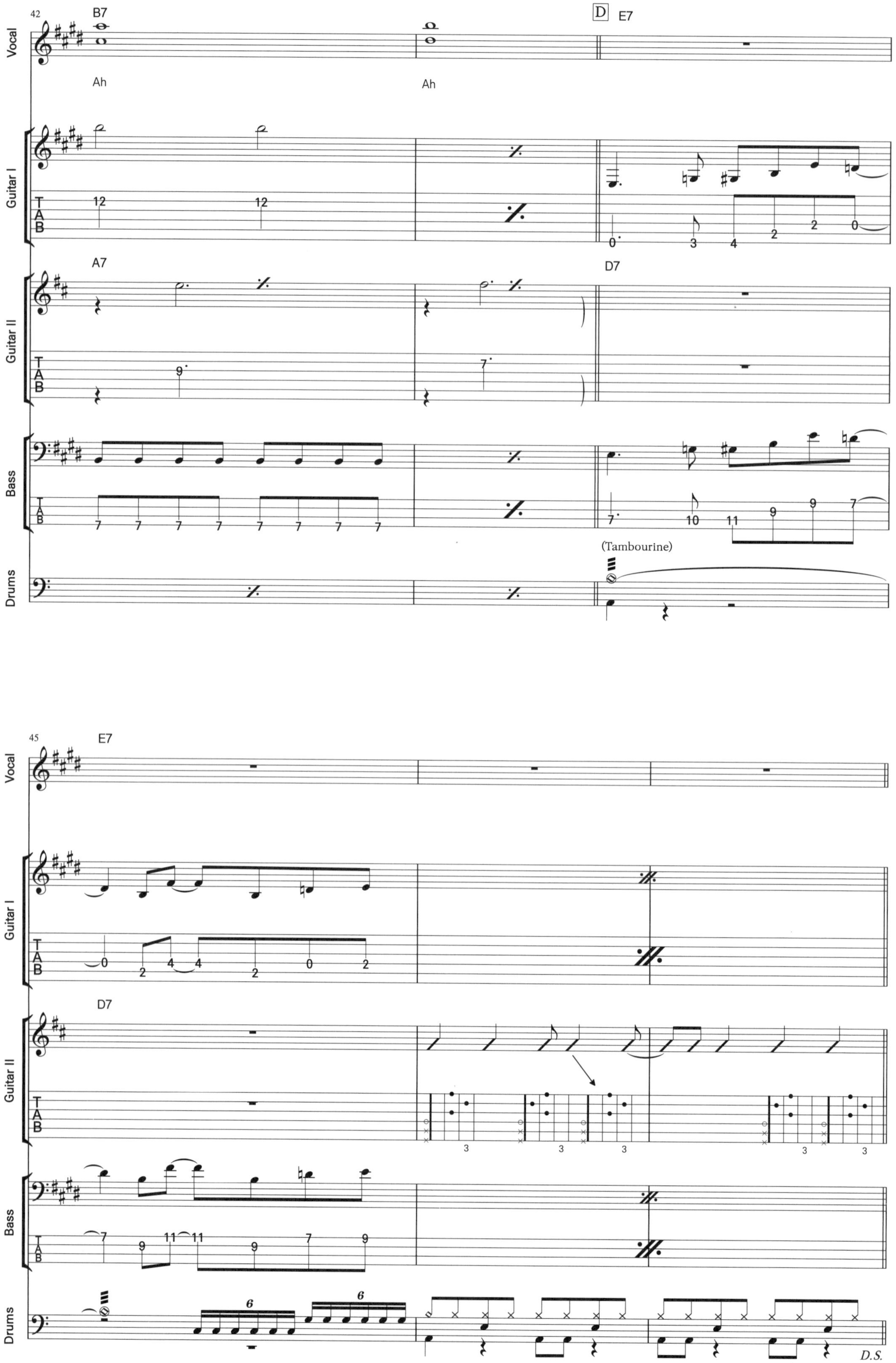

Vocal
Guitar I
Guitar II
Bass
Drums
B7
E7
A7
D7
E7
D7
Ah
Ah
(Tambourine)
D.S.

Coda
48
B7
E
E7
Vocal
Guitar I
out.
A7
D7
Guitar II
Bass
Drums
52
E7
Vocal
Guitar I
D7
Guitar II
Bass
(Tambourine)
Drums

Vocal
Guitar I
Guitar II
Bass
Drums
55
E7
F
E7
D7
D7
Day   Trip – per,
58
E7
D7
Day   Trip – per,   yeah.
Repeat & F.O.

# Taxman

Words & Music by
**George Harrison**

4
D7
D7(#9)
D7
Vocal
- will be -
- too small -
- it to -
- who die -
There's one -
Be thank -
If you -
Dec - lare -
Chorus
3. Ha ha - Mis - ter Wilson -
4. Tax - man - - - -
Guitar I
H
Guitar II
5
3 5
Bass
H
H
Drums

7
D7
D7(#9)
D7
Vocal
- for you, - nine - teen - for me -
- ful I - don't take - it all -
- don't want - to pay - some more -
- the pen - nies on - your eyes -
Chorus
Ha ha - Mis - ter Heath
Tax - man - - - -
Guitar I
H
H
Guitar II
4
4
Bass
H
Drums

B
C
'Cause I'm the Tax - man, yeah, -- I'm the
(1,2x tacet)
yeah, -- I'm the
H
H
H
H
3
Vocal
Chorus
Guitar I
Guitar II
Bass
Drums
G7
to D7
1.
2.
D7
Tax - man -
Tax - man -
Should five -
Now my -
If you drive -
Q.C
Q.C
H
H
(1,2x tacet)
(1,2x tacet)
H
H
H
H
H
5
3 5
3 5
5

C
17
D7
C7
Vocal
I'll  tax - the street          I'll  tax - your seat
Chorus
- a    car - car -    If you try - to sit - sit -    If you get -
Guitar I
Guitar II
Bass
H  P
Drums
21
D7
C7
Vocal
I'll  tax - the heat          I'll  tax - your feet -
Chorus
- too    cold - cold -    If you take - a walk - walk -
Guitar I
Guitar II
Bass
H  P
Drums

186

Tax – man!
Tax – man!

'Cause I'm the Tax - man,
yeah, - - I'm the Tax - man -
yeah, - - I'm the Tax - man -
Don't ask -
And you're - work - ing - for no-
Coda
D.S.
188

41
F7
F
D7
D7(#9)
D7
Vocal
- one    but me
Chorus
Tax - man - -
Guitar I
Guitar II
Bass
Drums
45
D7
D7(#9)
D7
Fade Out
189

# Eleanor Rigby

Words & Music by
John Lennon, Paul McCartney

Ah, — look at all — the lone — ly peo — ple
E – lea – nor Rig – by Picks up the rice – in the church – Where a wed – ding has been –
Fa – ther Mc – ken – zie Writ – ing the words – of a ser – mon That no – one will hear –
E – lea – nor Rig – by Died in the church and was buri – ed A – long – with her name –
3x only
2x
3x only

Vocal
Chrous
Violin I
Violin II
Viola I
Viola II
V.Cello
Em
C
Em
Lives in a dream
No - one comes near
No - bo - dy came
Waits at the win - dow
Look at him work - ing
Fa - ther Mc - Ken - zie
1x only
(3x only) 2x only
Em
Em7
C
Wear - ing the face that she keeps In a jar by the door
Darn - ing his socks in the night When there's no - bo - dy there
Wip - ing the dirt from his hands As he walks from the grave

192

Who is it for
What does he care
No – one was saved
All the lone – ly peo – ple
Where do –
ah, – look at all – the lone – ly peo –
3x only
(3x only)
(1x only)
– they all – come from
All the lone – ly peo –
– ple
Ah, – look at all –
2x only
193

24
Em6
C/E
to ⊕ 1. Em
Vocal
- ple    Where do - they - all be - long -
Chrous
- the lone - ly peo - ple
Violin I
Violin II
Viola I
Viola II
V.Cello
2. Em
27
Vocal
-
Chrous
Violin I
Violin II
Viola I
Viola II
V.Cello
D.C
⊕ Coda
Em
Vocal
-
Chrous
Violin I
Violin II
Viola I
Viola II
V.Cello

# Yellow Submarine



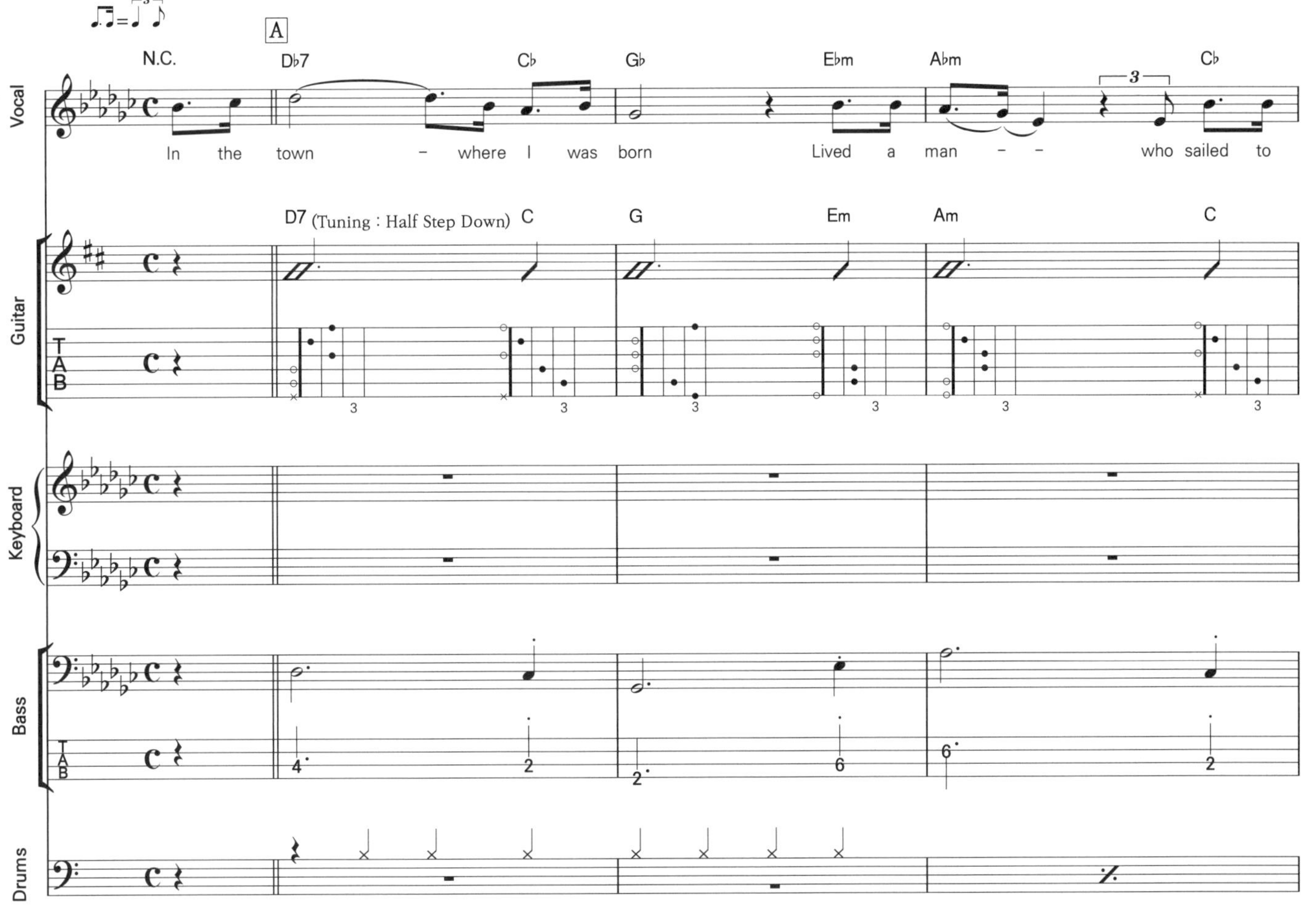

Vocal
Guitar
Keyboard
Bass
Drums
D♭7  G♭  D♭7  C♭  G♭  E♭m  A♭m  C♭
D7  G  D7  C  G  Em  Am  C
sea  And he told us of his life  In the land of sub-ma-
D♭7  G♭  D♭7  C♭  G♭  E♭m  C♭
D7  G  D7  C  G
-rines  So we sailed on to the sun  Till we
live  a life of ease  Eve-ry-

found – – the sea of green
– one of us has all we need
And we lived – be – neath the waves
Sky of blue – and sea of green
In our
In our
yellow – – sub – ma – rine
yellow – – sub – ma – rine
We all live in a

yel – low sub – ma – rine
Yel – low sub – ma – rine,
yel – low sub – ma – rine
We all live in a
yel – low sub – ma – rine
Yel – low sub – ma – rine,
yel – low sub – ma – rine And our friends – – are all a–
Vocal
Guitar
Keyboard
Bass
Drums
Db7
Gb
D7
G
Db7
Gb
D7
G
Db7
Cb
D7
C
1.
to Gb
D

Vocal
Guitar
Keyboard
Bass
Drums
26
Gb    Ebm  Abm      Cb    Db7      Gb    Db7      Cb
G     Em   Am       C     D7       G     D7       C
-board    Ma-ny more of them    live next door    And the band    -be-gins to-
(Brass)
30
Gb    Db7    Gb         Db7         Gb
G     D7     G          D7          G
-play-

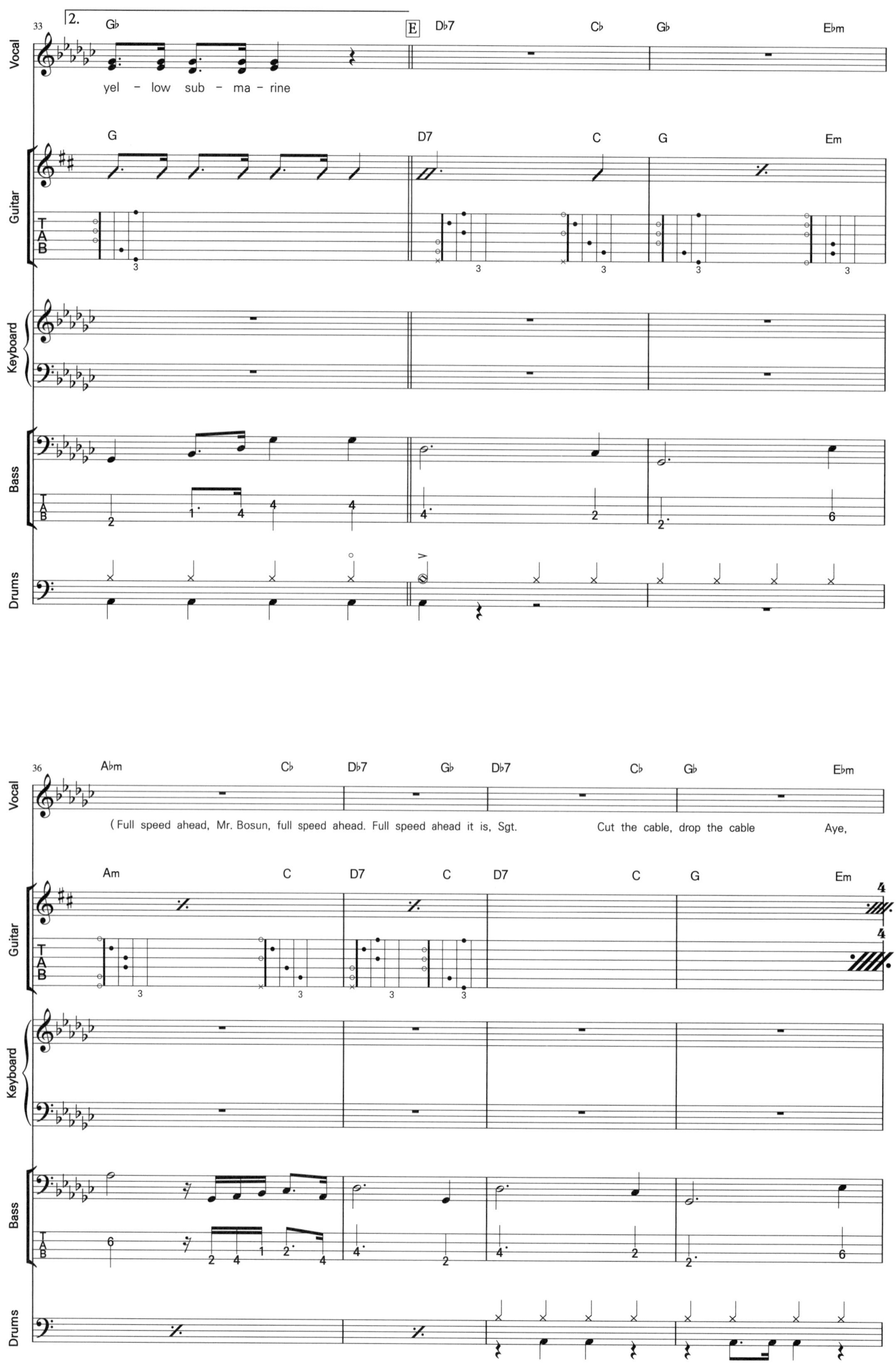
33
2.
E
Vocal
Guitar
Keyboard
Bass
Drums
G♭ D♭7 C♭ G♭ E♭m
yel - low sub - ma - rine
G D7 C G Em
36
A♭m C♭ D♭7 G♭ D♭7 C♭ G♭ E♭m
(Full speed ahead, Mr. Bosun, full speed ahead. Full speed ahead it is, Sgt. Cut the cable, drop the cable Aye,
Am C D7 C D7 C G Em

Sir, aye
Captain, Captain)  As we
yel – low sub – ma – rine
D.S.
Coda
We  all  live  in  a  yel – low  sub – ma – rine
Yel – low  sub – ma – rine
yel – low  sub – ma – rine
Repeat & F.O.

# Sgt. Pepper's Lonely Hearts Club Band

Words & Music by
John Lennon, Paul McCartney

twen-ty years a-go to-day — Ser-geant Pep-per taught the band to play — They've been go-ing in and out of style — but they're
real-ly want to stop the show — but I thought you might like to know — That the sing-er's going to sing a song — and he

gua-ran-teed to raise a smile — So may I in-tro-duce to you — the act you've known for all these years — —
wants you all to sing a-long — So let me in-tro-duce to you — the one and on-ly Bil-ly Shears — —

11
Vocal
Other
Guitar I
Guitar II
Bass
Drums
G7
C7
G7
to B
C7
2x(and) Ser–geant Pep – per's  Lone – ly Hearts – Club  Band
(Horn)
g
g
3  5
3
3  5
3  3  2  2  3  3  4  5
3  3  2  2  5  5  2  2
3  3  6  6  5  5  3  3
14
Vocal
Other
Guitar I
Guitar II
Bass
Drums
F7
C7
D7
We're
B
3  3  0  0  3  3  0  0  3  3  3  3  3  3  3  3
5  5  5  5
5  5  5  5

Ser – geant Pep – per's Lone – ly Hearts – Club Band – We hope you will en– joy – the show –
Ser – geant Pep – per's Lone – ly Hearts – Club Band – Sit back and let the eve – ning go

Ser - geant Pep - per's Lone - ly Ser - geant Pep - per's Lone - ly Ser -
- geant Pep - per's Lone - ly Hearts - Club Band - It's won - der - ful to be here it's

31
F7
C7
D7
Vocal
Other
Guitar I
Guitar II
Bass
Drums
cer - tain - ly a thrill You're such a love - ly au - di - ence we'd like to take you home with us we'd
3
3
1 1 0 0 3 3 0 3
3 3 6 6 5 5 3 3
5 5 5 5 5 5 2 5
34
D7
Coda
C7
Vocal
Other
Guitar I
Guitar II
Bass
Drums
love to take you home I don't
U D
U D
8 8 8
5 5 5 5
3 3 6 6 5 5 3 3
D.S.
Fade Out

# With A Little Help From My Friends



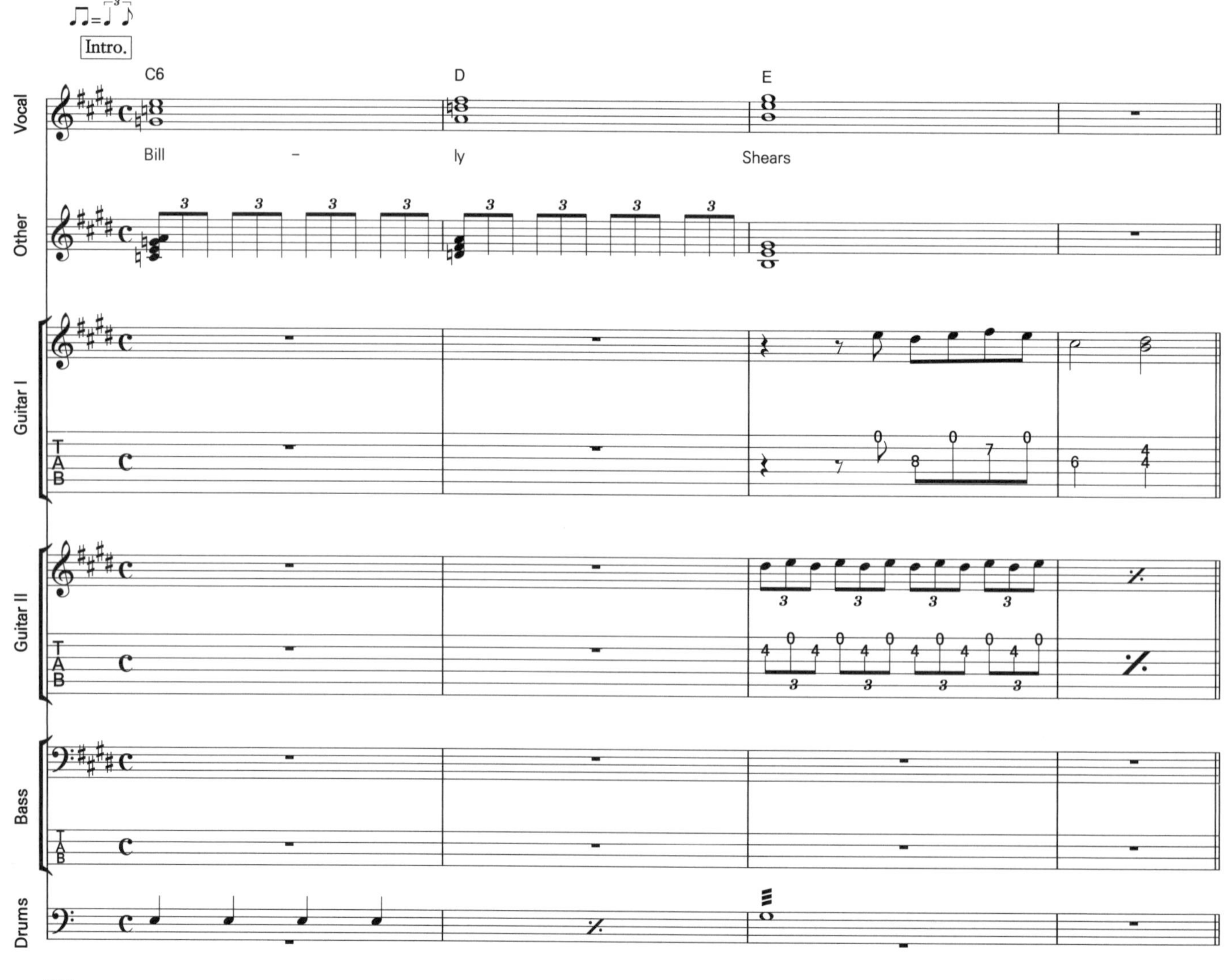

A
E          B          F#m7                    B7
What would you think – if I sang – out of tune – would you stand – up and walk – out on me –
E                              B          F#m7                    B7
Lend me your ears – and I'll sing – you a song – and I'll try – not to sing – out of key –
Vocal
Other
Guitar I
Guitar II
Bass
Drums

oh — I get by — with a lit-tle help — from my friends — Mm, — I get high —
— with a lit-tle help — from my friends — Mm, — I'm gon-na try — with a lit-tle help — from my friends —

What do I do - when my love -
- is a - way - does it wor - ry you to be a - lone -? How do I feel - by the end -

26
F#m7
B7
E
Vocal
Other
Guitar I
Guitar II
Bass
Drums
- of the day - are you sad - be-cause you're on your own - No - I got by -
29
D
D 3
3
A
E
D 3
3
A
1.2. - with a lit-tle help - from my friends - Mm, - I get high - with a lit-tle help - from my friends -
3. - with a lit-tle help - from my friends - Mm, - gon-na try - with a lit-tle help - from my friends -
Vocal
Other
Guitar I
Guitar II
Bass
Drums

Mm, — I'm gon na try — with a lit – tle help – from my friends – Do you need –
oh – – I get high – with a lit – tle help – from my friends –
a – ny – bo – dy? I need some – bo – dy to love –
I just need some – one to love –

Could it be — a-ny-bo-dy? I want some-bo-dy to love —
Would you be-lieve — in a love — at first sight — yes I'm car — tain that it hap-pens all the

time
What do you see – when you turn – out the light? – I can't tell
– you but I know – it's mine – oh – I get by – oh, – I get by –
2.
D.S.
215

Coda
52
Vocal
Yes – I get by – with a lit – tle help – from my friends – with a lit – tle help – from my friends
E
D
A
Other
Guitar I
Guitar II
Bass
Drums
55
Vocal
(Ah – – – – –)
C
D
E
Other
Guitar I
Guitar II
Bass
Drums

# Lucy In The Sky With Diamonds

Words & Music by
John Lennon, Paul McCartney

2x, D.S.time
A
Vocal
Other
Guitar I
Guitar II
Bass
Drums
Pic - ture your - self in a boat on a ri - ver with
Fol - low her down to a bridge by a fount - ain where
Pic - ture your - self on a train on a sta - tion with
A    A/G    A/F#    A/F
tan - ger - line trees and mar - ma - lade skies
rock - ing horse peo - ple eat marsh - mal - low pies
plast - i - cine port - ers with look - ing glass ties
A    A/G    A/F#    A/F

some - bo - dy calls - you, you an - swer quite
Eve - ry one smiles as you an drift past the
sud - den - ly some - one is there at the

slow - ly a girl with kal - eid - o - scope eyes.
flow - ers that grow so in - cred - ib - ly high.
turn - stile the girl with kal - eid - o - scope eyes.

21
A/F#
to Dm
Dm/C
Vocal
Other
Guitar I
Guitar II
Bass
Drums
B
24
Bb
C
Vocal
Cle - lo - phane flow - ers of yel - low and
News - pa - per tax - is ap - pear on the
Other
C U U U U D U
Guitar I
Guitar II
Bass
Drums
220

27
C
F
C
green tow – er – ing o – ver your
shore wait – ing to take you a –
U
U
C
U
U
U
U
U
U
C
U
U
U
U
U
3
30
Bb
C
head – Look for the girl
way – Climb in the back
U
D
C
U
U
U
D
C
U
U
3
3

with the sun in her eyes and she's gone
with your head in the clouds and you're gone
Lu – cy in the sky with dia – – monds, Lu – cy in the sky with
(2x with chorus)
(Organ)

dia - - monds,
Lu - cy in the sky - with dia - - monds,
Ah
Coda
Lu - cy in the sky - with
(Organ)
D.S.
223

Vocal
Other
Guitar I
Guitar II
Bass
Drums
dia - - monds,
Lu - cy in the sky - with dia - - monds,
Lu - cy in the sky - with dia - - monds,
Ah
Repeat & F.O.
224

# A Day In The Life

Words & Music by
John Lennon, Paul McCartney

A
G Bm Em Em7 C C/B
Vocal
Other
Piano
Guitar
Bass
Drums
I read the news - to-day - oh - boy
A - bout - a luck -y man - who
(Maracas)
Am9 G Bm Em Em7
made the grade -
And though the news - was ra - ther sad

Well I just had to laugh, - laugh - I saw the pho - to - graph - aph -
He blew his mind - out - in a car -
227

He did–n't no–tice that the lights had changed
A crowd of peo–ple stood and
stared
They'd seen his face be–fore –
No–bo–dy was really sure if he was from the House of Lords. –

I saw a film - to-day - oh - boy
The Eng-lish arm-y had just won the war
A crowd- of peo-ple turned a-way-

But I - just had to look -
Hav -ing read the
book
I'd love to turn - - - - - you - - - - on. - - - - - -
(Orchestra)

35
N.C.
Vocal
Other
Up and cresc.
Piano
Guitar
Bass
Drums
39
N.C.
Vocal
Other
Piano
Guitar
Bass
Drums

Vocal
Other
Piano
Guitar
Bass
Drums
N.C.
E
Woke up,
Cym. Fill
D
E
D
fell out of bed, dragged a comb a- cross my head. Found my
232

way down – stairs and drank a cup, and look – ing up – I no – ticed I was late. Ha, ha, ha. Found my
coat and grabbed my hat – made the bus in sec – onds flat. Found my

way up – stairs and had a smoke and some – bod – y spoke – and I went in – to a dream. – Ah
Ah – Ah – – – – Ah – –

Ah
Ah
I read the news today oh boy

four thou – sand holes – in Black – burn Lan –ca – shire
And though the holes – were rath – er
small
They had to count –them all –
Now they know how man – y holes it takes to fill the Al – bert Hall –

76
C
N.C.
I'd love to turn — — — — — you — — — — on. — — — —
Vocal
Other
Piano
Guitar
Bass
Drums
3
79
N.C.
Up and cresc.
3
3

82
N.C.
Vocal
Other
Piano
Guitar
TAB
Bass
TAB
Drums
86
N.C.
E
fff
238

# Magical Mystery Tour

Words & Music by
John Lennon, Paul McCartney

Step right this way!    1.2. Roll up, — — —    roll up — for the mys —
— te — ry tour —    Roll up, — — —    roll up — for the mys —
240

we've got ev - -ery - thing you need
- te - ry tour -    Roll   up -   and that's an   in - vi - ta - tion    Roll up - for the mys -
sa - tis - fac - tion guar - an - teed
- te - ry tour -    Roll up -    for make a   re - ser - va - tion    Roll up - for the mys -

The ma - gi - cal mys - te - ry tour is wait - ing to take you a
The ma - gi - cal mys - te - ry tour is hop - ing to take you a
- way
- way
Wait - ing to take you a - way
Hop - ing to take you a - way
- te - ry tour -

D
29
B
F#m7
Mys - te - ry  trip
Vocal
Other
Guitar I
Guitar II
Bass
Drums
roll
33
B
F#m7
G#m7
A
Vocal
Other
Guitar I
Guitar II
Bass
Drums
roll
roll
roll

Vocal
Other
Guitar I
Guitar II
Bass
Drums
Now
(Slow Down)
The ma - gi - cal mys -
- te - ry tour -
Roll up, -
roll up - for the mys -

and that's an in - vi - ta - tion
- te - ry tour -
Roll up, -
Roll up - for the mys -
to make a re - ser - va - tion
- te - ry tour -
Roll up, -
Roll up - for the mys -

A
F
D
D/C
- te - ry tour -
The ma - gi - cal mys - te - ry tour is
The ma - gi - cal mys - te - ry tour is
Vocal
Other
Guitar I
Guitar II
Bass
Drums
G/B
Gm/B♭
D/A
com - ing to take you a - way
dy - ing to take you a - way
com - ing to take you a
Dy - ing to take you a

Vocal
Other
Guitar I
Guitar II
Bass
Drums
way
way take you to day
roll
roll
roll
Dm7
247

67
Dm7
Vocal
Other
Guitar I
TAB
Guitar II
TAB
Bass
TAB
Drums
71
Dm7
Vocal
Other
Guitar I
TAB
Guitar II
TAB
Bass
TAB
Drums
roll
roll
Fade Out

# The Fool On The Hill

Words & Music by
John Lennon, Paul McCartney

Em7/D
D6
lone       on   a   hill
ad        in   a   cloud
The  man  with  the  fool  –  ish
The  man  of   a   thou  –  sand
Vocal
Other
Piano
Guitar
Bass
Drums
D6
Em7/D
grin   is     keep  –  ing   per  –  fect  –  ly  –  still   –
voic  –  es   talk  –  ing   per  –  fect  –  ly  –  loud   –
But
But
(1x tacet)
(1x tacet)

(Straight)
B  Em7        A7        D6
no - bo - dy wants - to know - him   they can see - that he's just a fool -
no - bo - dy ev - er hears - him     on the sound - he ap - pears to make -
no - bo - dy seems - to like - him   they can tell - what he wants to do -
(Harmonica)
Bm7        Em7        A7
- And he ne - ver gives an ans - wer    But the fool -
- And he ne - ver seems to no - tice
- And he ne - ver shows his feel - ings
(Harmonica)

17
Dm
Dm(#5)
Dm
Dm(#5)
Vocal
Other
Piano
Guitar
Bass
Drums
— — on the hill — sees the sun — go-ing down — And the eyes—
(Shaker)
(Bell)
21
C7
Dm
— in his head — see the world — spin-ning round —

252

Vocal
Other
Piano
Guitar
Bass
Drums
24
Dm7
D6
D.S. time
oh
C
27
D6
Em7/D
(Flute 2)
(Flute 1)
1x tacet
1x tacet
253

31
Vocal
Other
Piano
Guitar
Bass
Drums
D6
Em7/D
to
round
round
round
round
round
3
3
4
4
1x tacet
1x tacet
2
0
2
0
3
34
Em7/D
Coda
Em7/D
D
Em7
And
And    He    ne - ver    lis - tens    to
(Harmonica)
5
5
D.S.

37
A7
D6
Bm7
Vocal
Other
Piano
Guitar
TAB
Bass
TAB
Drums
- them   He   knows   that   they're -   the   fool - -
40
Em7
A7
Dm
Dm(#5)
they   do - n't   like   him   The   fool -   on   the   hill -
(Harmonica)

sees the sun - going down - And the eyes - in his head -
see the world - spin - ning round -

51
D6
D6
Em7/D
Vocal
oh
round
round
Other
(Flute 2)
(Flute 1)
Piano
Guitar
Bass
Drums
55
Em/D
D
Em7/D
round
round
oh
Fade Out
257

# I Am The Walrus

Words & Music by
John Lennon, Paul McCartney

1. I am he as you are he as
2. Mis-ter ci-ty police-man sit-ting
3. Ex-pert tex-pert chok-ing smok-ers

you are me and we are all to-ge-ther
Pret-ty lit-tle police-man in a row
Don't you think the jo-ker laugh at you

See how thoy run like pigs from a gun See
See how they fly like Lu-cy in the sky See
See how they smile like pigs in a sty See

Chorus D.S.2. time
Ho ho ho, hee hee hee, ha ha ha

12
Vocal
D
A
1.
B  A  A/G
how – they fly –  I'm cry – – ing –
how – they run –  I'm cry – – ing –
how – they snied –  I'm cry – – ing –
(1.) Sit –ting on  a corn – flake
I'm (D.S.1) Yel –low mat –ter cus – tard
(D.S.2) Sem – o – li – na pil – chards
Other
Horn 1x
Horn D.S.1.time
Piano
2x
2x
Other
D.S.2.time
Bass
5  5  5  5 5 5 5
7
7  7  7 7 5 5 5
Drums
15
Vocal
D9/F#  F  G  A  A/G  F
Wait – ing  for the van  to come – –
Drip – ping from a dead dog's  eye –
climb – ing  up the Eif – fel  Tow –er
Cor – po – ra – tion tee shirt Stu –pid  bloo – dy Tues – day Man –
Crab – a – lock – er fish –wife  por – no – graph – ic  pries –tess Boy –
El – e – men– tary pen –guin  sing – ing  Ha – re Khrish – na
Other
Piano
Other
Bass
4 4 4  3  3  5
7  7 7  5 5 5
3  3  3 3 3  3  3
Drums

260

B
- you been a naugh-ty boy - You let your face grow long
- you been a naugh-ty girl - You let your knick-ers down -
Man you should have seen them Kick-ing Ed-gar Al - lan Poe -
C
I am the egg-man, they are the
(Chorus)
Hu
D.S.1.2.time
D
egg-men
E
I am the wal-rus, goo goo g' joob
D.S.2 (joob goo goo)
to 1.2. C
Dsus4
cry -
Hu
D.S. 2.time
Hu
(Chorus)
Hu -
D.S.2.time

24
Dsus4
A
E
D
Vocal
- - ing I'm cry - - ing I'm cry - ing
Other
(Melotoron)
Piano
Other
Bass
Drums
D.S. 1.
Coda 1.
28
E
D
B
A
G
F
E
Vocal
Other
(Bell)
Piano
Other
Bass
Drums
262

Sit - ting in an Eng - lish gar - den wait - ing for the sun - If the sun don't
come, you get a tan from stand - ing in the Eng - lish rain - I am the egg - man, they are the

38
D    E    D
Vocal
egg-men    I am the wal-rus,    goo goo g' joob g' goo - goo g' joob -
Other
Piano
Other
Bass
Drums
D.S.2.

Coda 2.
41
D    C    B    F  A
2x tacet
Vocal
- goo g' joob -    Goo goo g' goog' goo - goo g' joob goo -    ju-ba ju-ba ju-ba    ju-ba    ju-ba    ju-ba
Other
Hu    -    -    (Rhythmical Speaking)
Piano
Other
Bass
Drums

264

ju-ba    ju-ba    ju-ba  ju-ba    ju-ba  ju-ba
(Speaking)
Oompah, oompah, stick it up your jumper!    Oompah, oompah, stick it up your jumper!
Everybody's got one, everybody's got one    Everybody's got one, everybody's got one    Everybody's got one, everybody's got one
Repeat &F.O.

# Hello Goodbye

Words & Music by
**John Lennon, Paul McCartney**

Am    G7    Am    G7
- say go - go go -
- say I - don't know -
Oh - no -
1H.U  D
1H.U  D
10    10
P
P
7 5 3 2  5 3 2  5  3 5 2 5  5 3 5 7 5 3 2 0  3 5 2 5  2 5
G7    C/G    G7    F/G    B    C    C/B
You say - good bye - and I say hel - lo - Hel - lo - hel - lo
(Chorus)
2x only Hel - lo Good - bye Hel - lo Good - bye -
2x tacet
2x tacet
3 5  2 3 5  2  4 5
5  5  3 3 2 2
2x

I don't know why you say good bye I say hello
Hel-lo Good-bye
Hel-lo hel-lo
Hel-lo Good-bye Hel-lo Good-bye
I don't know why you say good bye I say hel-lo
Hel-lo Good-bye
Hel-lo Good-bye
2x
to 1.2.
1.
(2x tacet)

Why why why why why why - do you say -
good-bye - good-bye - bye bye bye bye Oh - no - -
(Organ)
echo
1H.U D

Coda 1.
25
G7   C/G   G7   F/G
Vocal
You say - good bye - and I say hel - lo -
Other
Piano
Guitar
Bass
Drums
D.S. 1.
E
28
F6   C   G7   Am
Vocal
You say yes - I say no - You say stop - and I say go - go - go-
Other
(Chorus)
(Organ)
I say yes - but I may mean no - I can stay - till it's time to
Piano
Guitar
Bass
Drums

Vocal
Other
Piano
Guitar
Bass
Drums
(Fiddle)
go
G7
Am
G7
G
C/G
G7
Ah
Oh - no -
You say - good -bye - and
F/G
I     say   he - llo -
Coda 2.
C
C/B
Am7
Am7/G
- hel - lo - hel lo - -
I don't - know
(Organ)
D.S.2.

Vocal
Other
Piano
Guitar
Bass
Drums
39
F
Ab6
Cm/G
D/F#
F
why you say - good - bye  I say hel - lo  —  —  —  —  —  —  —  —  —  Hel -
C
F
C
2x (cha  cha  cha)
- lo  —  —  —
Hey  la,  hey  — a - lo - ha
(Chorus)
Hey  la,  hey  — a - lo - ha
3x
3x ( Ooo  — )
C  U
C  U
Repeat & F.O.
272

# Strawberry Fields Forever

Words & Music by
John Lennon, Paul McCartney

5
A   B♭
Fm7
Vocal
Upper part D.S.2.time only
1.,2.,3.,4. Let me take you down – 'cause I'm go – in' to Straw – ber – ry
Guitar
S
S
Other
D.S.2.time
Other
1.2x only
Bass
1.2x only
(1.2x only)
1x only
1x only
Drums
(Dubbing Bass Tom)
2x,D.S.1.2.time
8
Fm7
G7
Vocal
Fields.
Noth – ing is real, and
Guitar
S
H
S
H
S
Other
(D.S.2.time)
D.S.1.2.time
Other
(1,2x only)
1x only
Bass
Drums

Vocal
Guitar
Other
(Trumpet)
Other
Bass
Drums
11
Eb
G7
Eb
to 2.
1.
Bb
2x,D.S.1.2.time
(2x,D.S.1.2.time)
noth -ing  to  get    hung a- bout, –    Straw -ber -ry Fields – for  –  e - ver.
H
%  1.2. (D.S.time with Repeat)
15
B
F
F7
Gm
Gm/F
Liv – ing   is   ea – sy  with   eyes    closed, –   Mis – un –der –stand –ing all you
No  one  I   think  is   in    my    tree  –   I  mean  it  must  be  high  or
Al – ways  know,  some – times think  it's   me,  –   But you know  I   know when it's  a
D.S.1.2.time
1x only
1x only
g
H

see. It's get-ting hard to be some-one but it all works out,
low. That is, you know you can't tune in but it's all right
dream. I think a "No" will be a "Yes," but it's all wrong

It does-n't mat-ter much to me.
that is, I think it's not too bad.
that is, I think I dis-ag-ree.
- e - ver.

(D.S.1.time)
(D.S.1.2.time)
(1x only)
to

Coda 1.
Coda 2.
-e - ver,
D.S.1.
D.S.2.
Straw - ber - ry Fields - for - e - ver,
Straw - ber - ry Fields - for - e - ver
U D
U D

31
Vocal
Guitar
Other
Other
Bass
Drums
Eb
C
Bb
Bb/Ab
Bb
H P
HP
(Piano)
(Dubbing Bass Drum)
35
Bb
Eb
Bb
Bb/Ab
tr.
tr.

Vocal
Guitar
Other
Other
Bass
Drums
40
Bb
Bb
45
D
N.C.
(Tape Reverse)
(Dubbing Bass Drum)
Fade Out
Fade In
279

49
Vocal
N.C.
Guitar
W.H.C  U  U  U
W.H.C  U  U  U
14 11 11 11 11
14 14 14 14
Other
(Piano)
Other
Bass
Drums
54
N.C.
Vocal
Guitar
Other
3  3
Other
Bass
Drums
Fade Out

# Penny Lane

Words & Music by
John Lennon, Paul McCartney

3
Vocal
B
Bm7
Bm6/G#
– he's had the plea – sure to – know – And all the peo – ple that come and go –
Other
(8va)
Piano
Bass
9 8 6 4
2.
6
Drums 
o +
6
GM7
F#7sus4
F#7
F#7sus4
F#7
– Stop and say – hel – lo – On the
(8va)
3
3
3
5
4.
4 4 4
o + o + o +
282

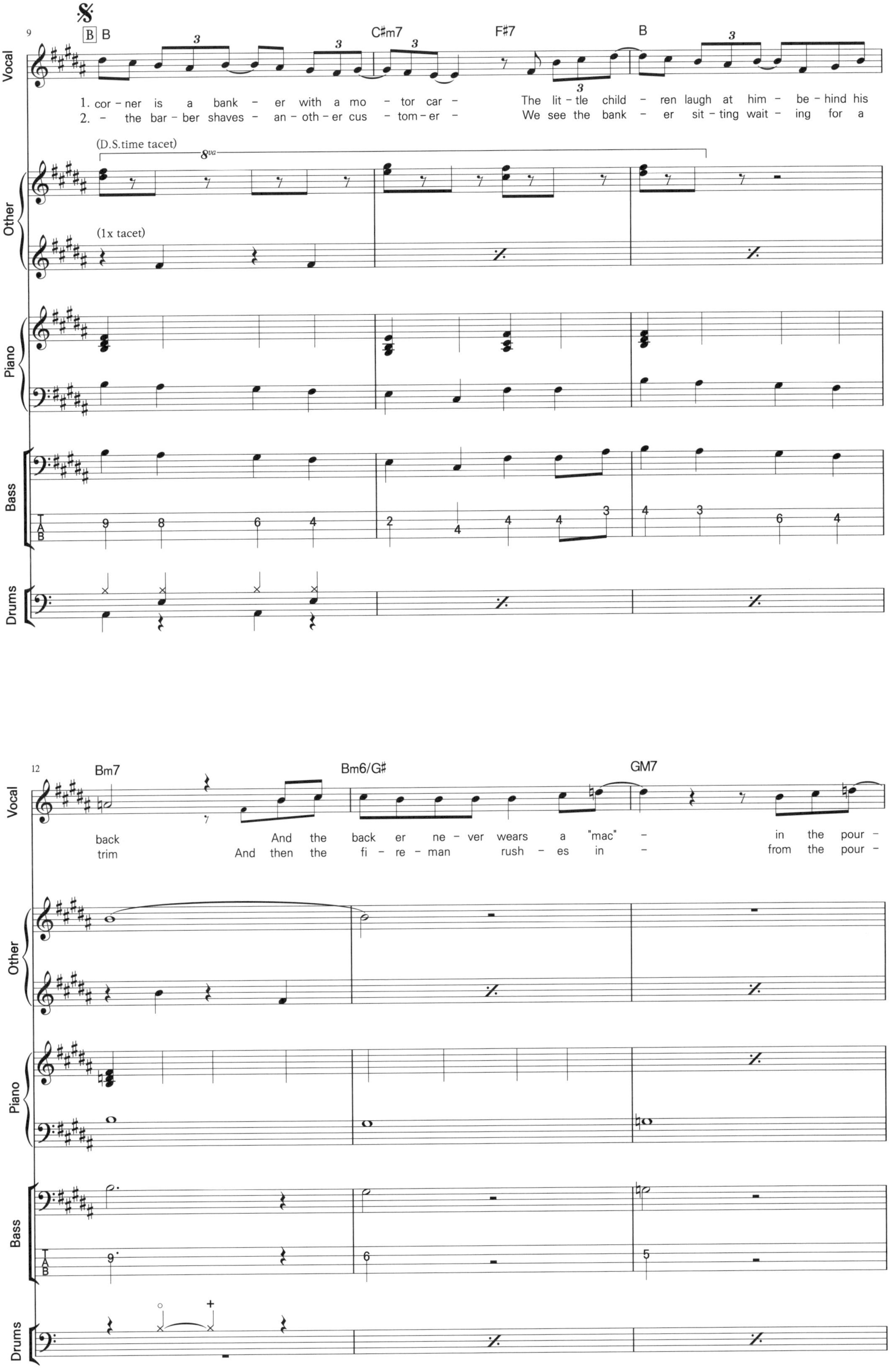
B B C#m7 F#7 B
Vocal
1. cor – ner is a bank – er with a mo – tor car – The lit – tle child – ren laugh at him – be – hind his
2. – the bar – ber shaves – an – oth – er cus – tom – er – We see the bank – er sit – ting wait – ing for a
(D.S.time tacet)
8va
(1x tacet)
Other
Piano
Bass
Drums
Bm7 Bm6/G# GM7
back And the back er ne – ver wears a "mac" – in the pour –
trim And then the fi – re – man rush – es in – from the pour –

Vocal
Other
Piano
Bass
Drums
F#7sus4
F#7
E
3
C
A
- ing rain
- ing rain
Ve - ry strange -
Ve - ry strange -
Pen - ny Lane (1.3.) -
Pen - ny lane (2.) -
is in my
is in my
ears -
ears -
3
D.S.time
A/C#
D
D/A
2x.D.S.time
(D)
- and in my eyes -
- and in my eyes -
D.S.time
Vocal
Other
Piano
Bass
Drums

Vocal
A
A/C#
D
to [coda]
There be - neath the blue – sub - ur - ban skies – I sit and
Full of fish – and fin - ger pies – in sum - mer
Other
D.S.time
D.S.time
D.S.time
Piano
Bass
Drums
mean - while back In Pen - ny Lane – there is a fire - man with an bo - ur glass – And in his pock-
mean - while back Be -hind the shel – ter in the mid - dle of the round - a bout – The pret - ty nurse-
F#7
D
B
C#m7
F#7
(2x tacet)
(1x tacet)

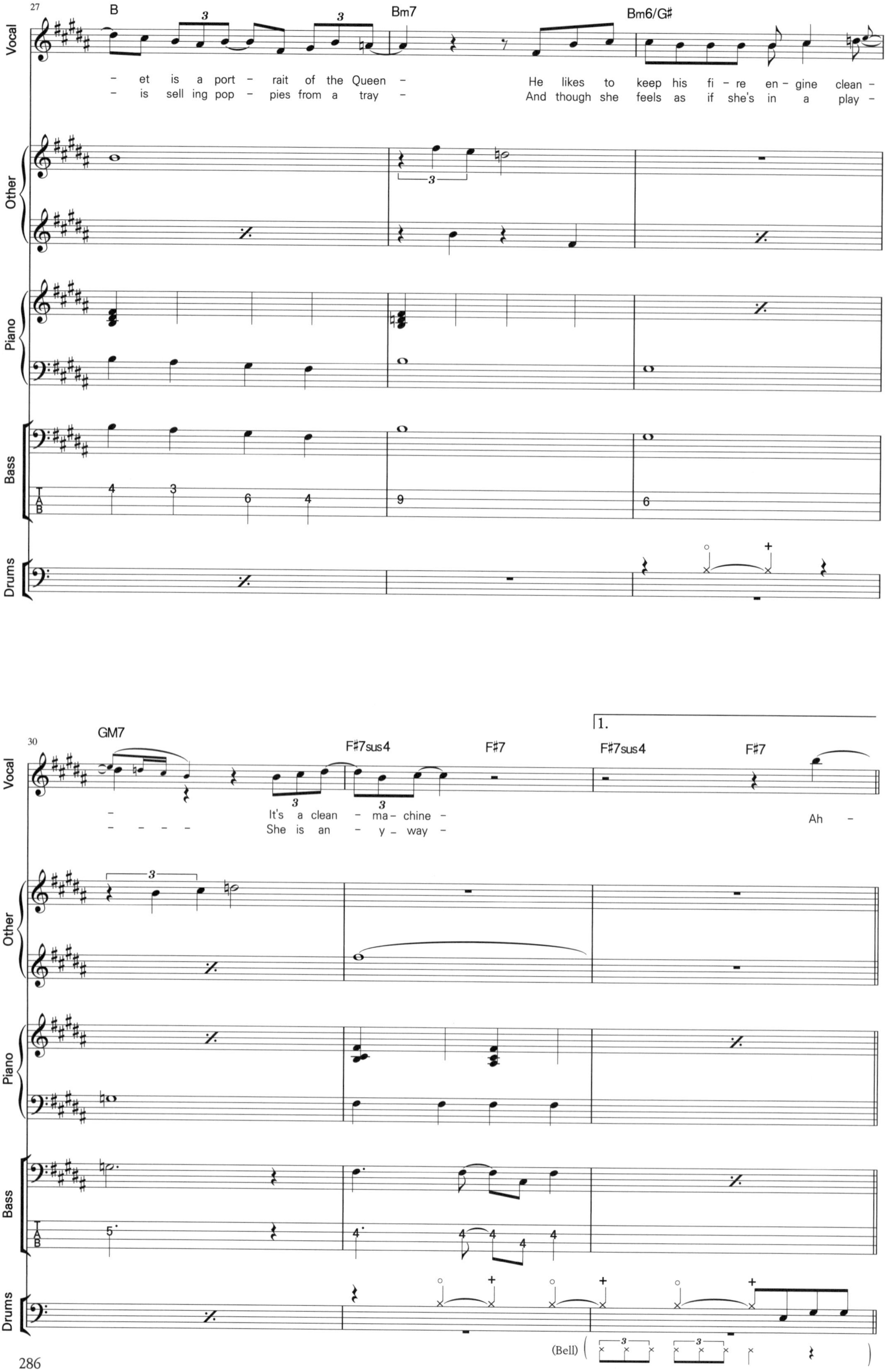
27
B
Bm7
Bm6/G♯
Vocal
– et is a port – rait of the Queen –
– is sell ing pop – pies from a tray –
He likes to keep his fi – re en – gine clean –
And though she feels as if she's in a play –
Other
Piano
Bass
T A B
Drums
30
GM7
F♯7sus4
F♯7
1.
F♯7sus4
F♯7
– It's a clean – ma – chine –
– – – – She is an – y – way –
Ah –
(Bell)

287

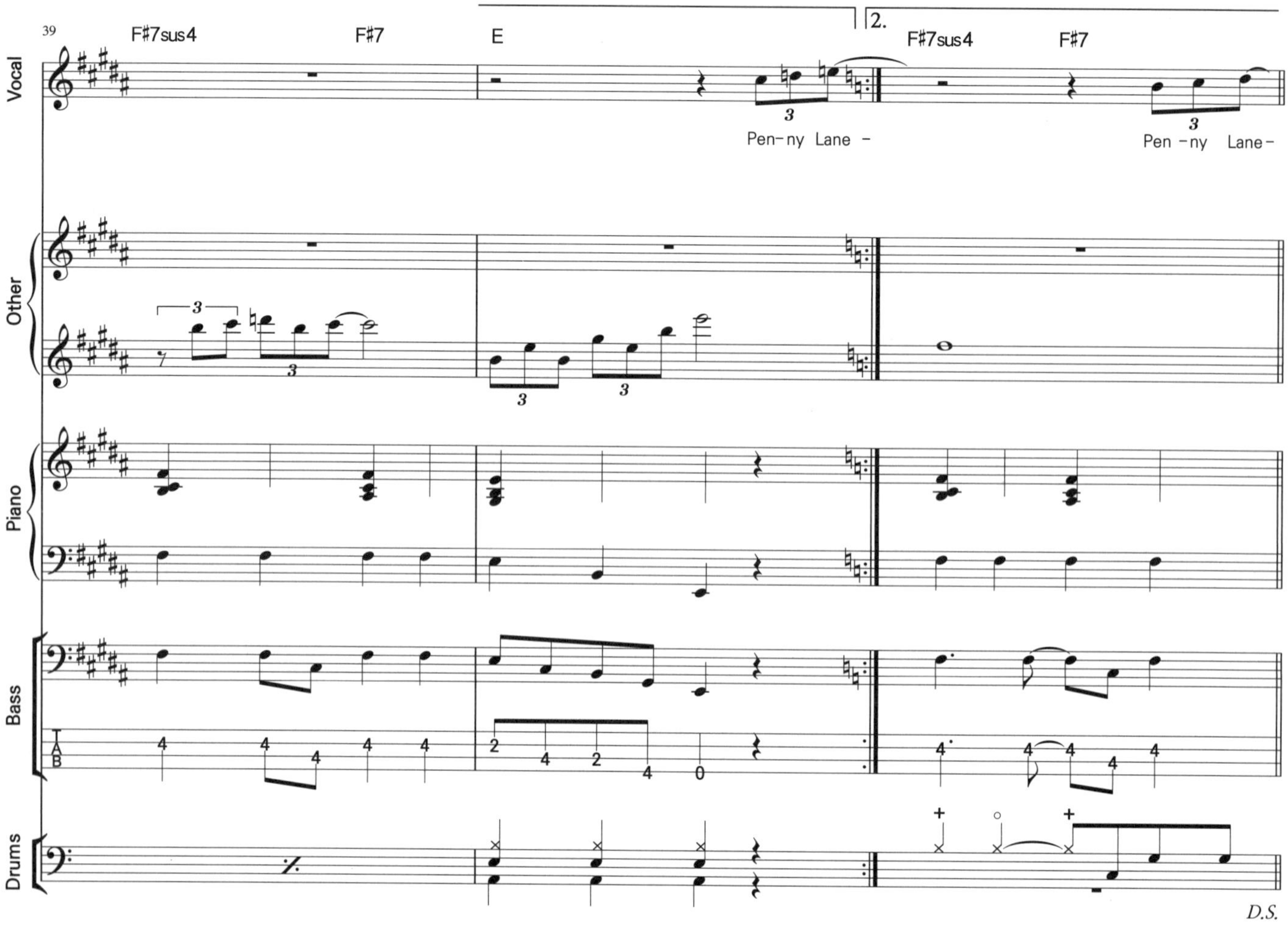
39
F♯7sus4
F♯7
E
2.
F♯7sus4
F♯7
Vocal
Pen-ny Lane -
Pen -ny Lane-
Other
Piano
Bass
Drums
D.S.

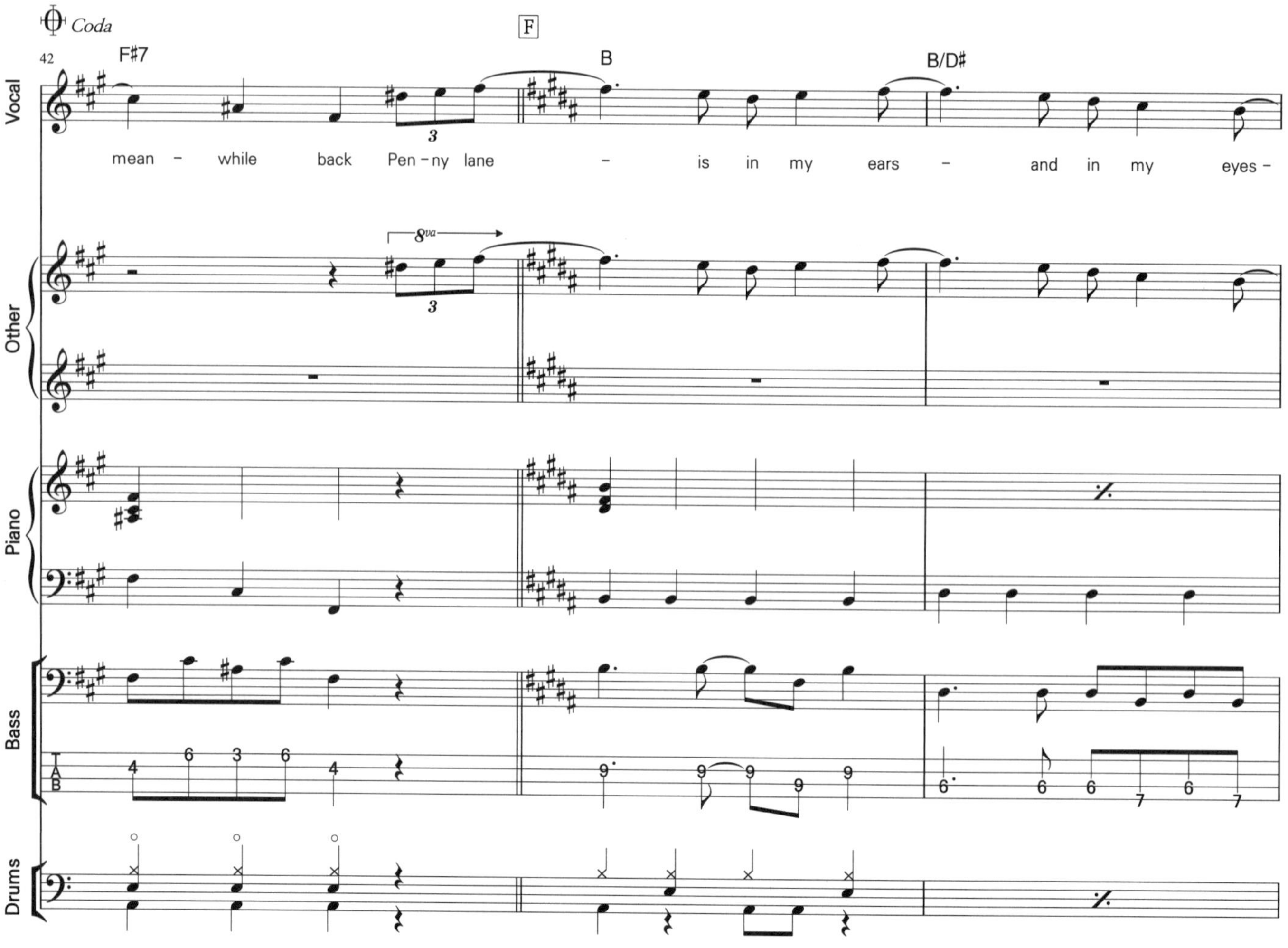
Coda
F
42
F♯7
B
B/D♯
Vocal
mean - while back Pen-ny lane - is in my ears - and in my eyes -
Other
8va
Piano
Bass
Drums

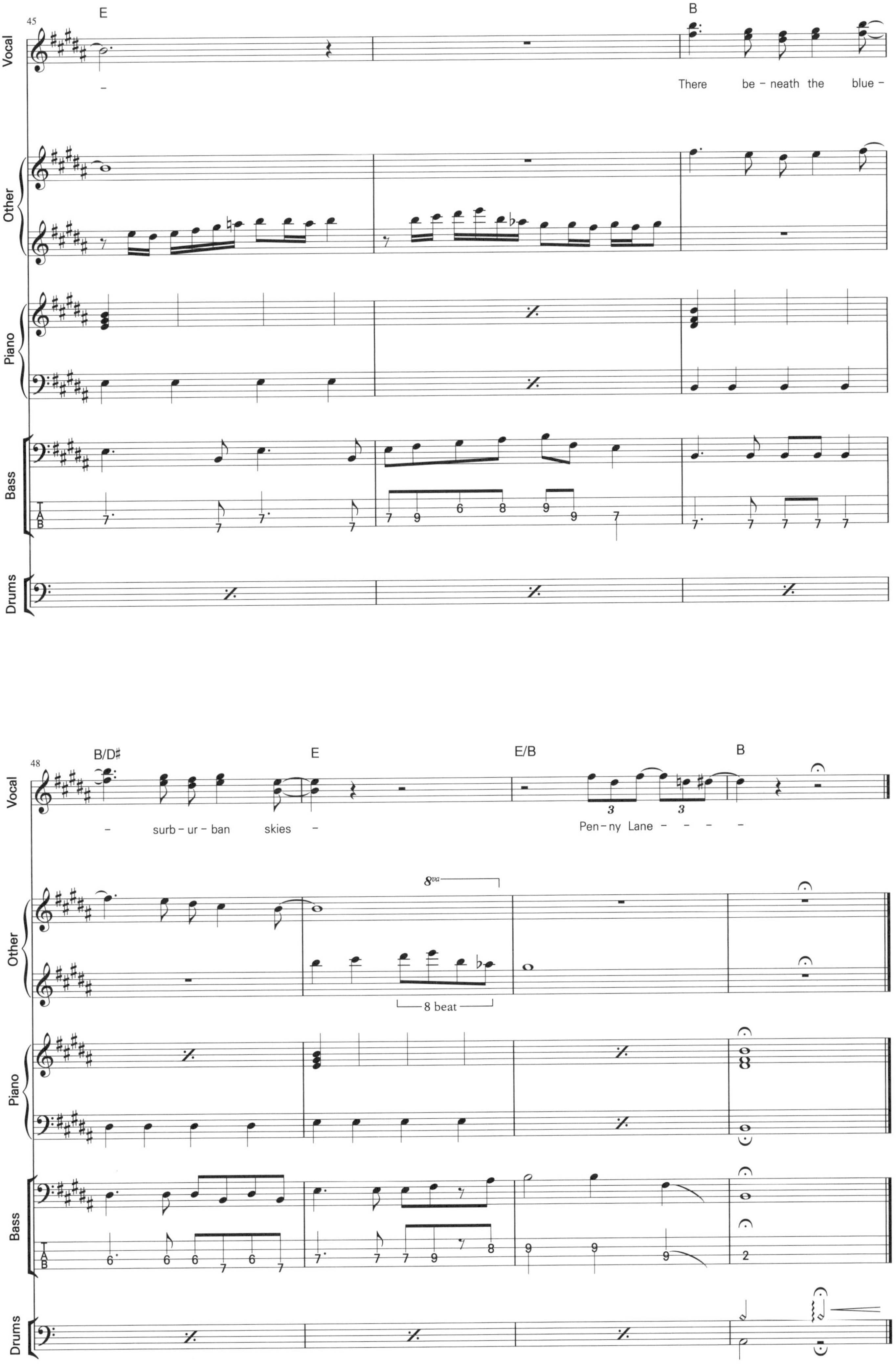

Vocal
Other
Piano
Bass
Drums
E
B
There be – neath the blue –
B/D#
E
E/B
B
surb – ur – ban skies –
Pen – ny Lane – – – –
8va
8 beat
289

# All You Need Is Love

Words & Music by
John Lennon, Paul McCartney

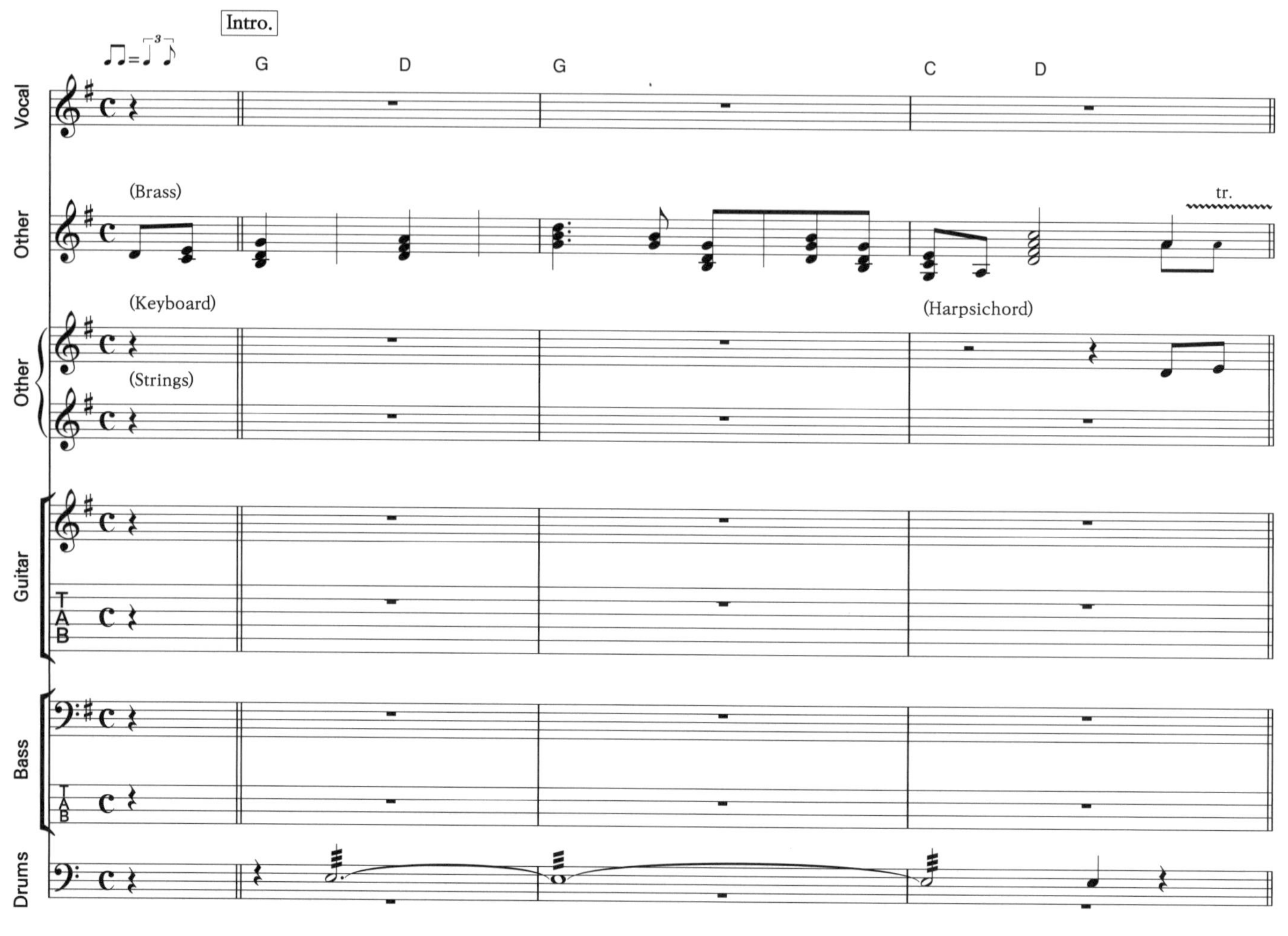

A
Vocal
Other
Other
Guitar
TAB
Bass
TAB
Drums
G
D
Em
G
D
Em
Love
love
love
Love
love
love
Am7
G
D
Love
love
love
(Cello)

(Chorus) 12
B
1.(Straight)
Vocal
Other
Other
(Violin)
1x tacet
Guitar
Bass
Drums
G Ah
D/F#
Em
G Ah
D/F#
There's no – thing you can do that can't be done –
No – thing you can make that can't be made –
No – thing you can know that is – n't known –
No – thing you can sing that can't be
No – one you can save that can't be
No – thing you can see that is – n't
15
Em
Am7 Ah
G
D/F#
D/E
sung –
saved –
shown –
No – thing you can say but you can learn – how to play the game – It's
No – thing you can do but you can learn – how to be you in time – It's
No – where you can be That is – n't where–(you're) mea – nt to be – – It's
292

𝄋 2.
C  G  A7
(Upper Part D S 1 2 time)
All you need is love -
ea - sy
ea - sy
ea - sy
1x only
(1x tacet)
18
D  D/C  D/B  D
Vocal
Other
Other
Guitar
Bass
Drums
D.S.2. time
21
D7
All to - ge - ther
G  A7  D7
Ev - ery - bo - dy
All you need is love -
Vocal
Other
Other
Guitar
Bass
Drums

24
Vocal
Other
Other
Guitar
Bass
Drums
G
B7
Em
Em7/D
CM7
D7
(Upper Part D.S.1.2.time)
(Middle Part 2x,D.S.1.2.time)
to 1.2.
All you need is love, — love, —
Love is all — you need —
(Cello)
1x tacet
(1x tacet)
3
3
3
3
3
3
3
3
1.
27
D
G
G
D/F#
Em
G
D/F#
Love
love
love
Love
Love
(1x only)
(E.Guitar)
C
U D C
C D
C D
C U D C U D
A.Guitar B 1-5 Col
C
U D C
C D
C U D C U D

love
Love
love
love
(A.Guitar)
2.
D.S.1.

Coda 1.
Coda 2.
E
Love is all - you need
Love is all - you need
Love is all - you need
Love is all - you need
Love is all - you need
- you need
love is all - you need
love is all - you need
love is all -
D.S.2.
Repeat & F.O.

# Back In The U.S.S.R.

Vocal
Other
Guitar I
Guitar II
Bass
Drums
Perc.
E7
A
D
Oh
Flew in from Miami Beach B. O. A. C. Didn't
Been away so long I hardly knew the place Gee
me round your snow peaked mountains way down south Take
(Jet)
(A.Piano)
D.S.x only, 8va
D.S.x only
D.S.x only
(Hand Clap)
C
D
get to bed last night On
it's good to be back home Leave
me to your daddy's farm Let
298

Vocal
Other
Guitar I
Guitar II
Bass
Drums
Perc.

A
D
C

- the way the pa-per bag was on my knee - Man - I had a dread-ful fight
- it till to-mor-row to un-pack my case - Ho - ney dis-con-nect the phone
- me hear your ba-la-lai-ka's ring-ing out - Come - and keep your com-rade warm

D.S.x

D
A
C

I'm back in the U. S. S. R. -
I'm back in the U. S. S. R. -
I'm back in the U. S. S. R. - Hey

You don't know how luc-ky you are -
You don't know how luc-ky you are -
You don't know how luc-ky you are -

(D.S.x only,8va)
(Gt.3.)
(D.S.x only)
(Gt.3.)

H

16
D
to
1.
A
Vocal
boy
boy
boy
Back - in the U. S. S. R. -
Yeah
Other
Guitar I
Guitar II
Bass
Drums
Perc.

19
B7
E7
2. N.C.
Vocal
Back - in the U. S. Back - in the U. S. Back - in the
Other
Guitar I
Guitar II
Bass
Drums
Perc.

22
Vocal
N.C.
A
A7
B D7
wu
(Upper Part Chorus)
(Lower Part Chorus)
dan dan dan dan dan dan dan
Well the Uk - raine girls real - ly
Other
U. S. S. R.
Guitar I
Guitar II
Bass
Perc. Drums
26
D7
wu
wu
A
A7
dan dan dan dan dan dan dan dan dan dan
knock me out - They leave the - West be - hind - And
Guitar I
Guitar II
Bass
Drums
Perc.

Vocal
Other
Guitar I
Guitar II
Bass
Drums
Perc.
D
D/C#
D/C
B7
E7
wu
wu
wu
dan dan
dan dan
dan dan
dan dan
dan
dan
dan
dan
Mos - cow girls make me sing out shout - That Geor gia's al - ways on my my my
(H.H. Poco Open)
D7
A
B7
E7
dan
dan
dan
dan
my my my my my my - - mind
oh - Come on
302

C
35
A
D
C
D
Hu Hey
Hu Hey
AH –
Vocal
Other
Guitar I
Guitar II
Bass
Drums
Perc.
39
A
D
C
D
– yeah
Yeah Yeah
Yeah – I'm back in the U. S. S. R.–
Vocal
Other
Guitar I
Guitar II
Bass
Drums
Perc.

D
You don't know how luc-ky you are - boys -
Back - in the U. S. S. R. -
(Lower Part Chorus)
dan dan dan
Well the
(Gt.3.)
(Gt.3.)

2.
49
Vocal
mind    Oh - - show -
Back - in the U. S. S. R.-
Other
gliss.
gliss.
Guitar I
Guitar II
Bass
Perc. Drums
D.S.
Coda
D
52
A        B7       E7       A
Vocal
- oh - let me tell you ho-ney
(Shouting)
Other
Guitar I
8va
(Gt.3.)
(Gt.3.)
H
H    H
Guitar II
Bass
Perc. Drums
E
305

55
A
Vocal
Other
Guitar I
Guitar II
Bass
Perc. Drums
wu
H
58
A
Vocal
Other
Guitar I
Guitar II
Bass
Perc. Drums

# Ob-La-Di, Ob-La-Da

Words & Music by
John Lennon, Paul McCartney

1. (Straight)
2.
A
Bb    F7
D.S.2.x
Des – mond has a bar – row in the mar – ket place – Mol –
Des – mond takes a trol – ley to the jewel – ler's store – Buys –
Hap – py ev – er af – ter in the mar – ket place – des –
Hap – py ev – er af – ter in the mar – ket place – Mol –
A
A
E7
F7    Bb
– ly is the sin – ger in a band
– a twen – ty ca – rat gol – den ring (rin – ring – )
– mond lets the child – ren lend a hand
– ly lets the child – ren lend a hand
Des – mond says to Mol – ly "Girl, I
Takes – it back to Mol – ly wait – ing
Mol – ly stays at home and does her
Des – mond stays at home and does his
E7
A

Vocal
Eb          Bb          F7          Bb
(Chorus 2x) Ob – la – di
like your face" – And Mol – ly says this as she takes him by the hand
at the door – And as he gives it to her she be – gins to sing
pre – tty face – And in the eve – ning she still sings it with the hand
pre – tty face – And in the eve – ning she's a sin – ger with the hand
(sin – sing) Ob – la – di –
(Yeah)
Other
D.S.1.2.x
(Brass)
Piano
Guitar
D          A          E7          A
Bass
Drums
Perc.
Bb          Dm7/F          Gm7          Bb          F7
B  La La La La La La La La La La La La – La – La how the life goes on –
– Oh – la – da – life goes on – bra – La – la how the life goes on –
A          C#m7/E          F#m7          A          E7

Vocal
Other
Piano
Guitar
Bass
Perc. Drums
17
Bb
Dm7/F
Gm7
La La La La La La La La La La La La La
Ob - la - di - Oh - la - da - life goes on - bra - La -
A
C#m7/E
F#m7
3
5
3
1 5 3 1 5 3
3 5 3 5 5 3
20
Bb
F7
to 2.
1.
Bb
2.3.
Bb
Bb7
- la how the life goes on
- la how the life goes on - - Yeah - -
gliss.
A
E7
A
A
A7
3
3
3
3
3
1 5 3 5 3
1 5 1 5 3
1 0 3 3 4 0
5
310

C
23
Eb
Bb
(Ab/Bb)
Vocal
In a couple of years they have built a home sweet home –
Other
Piano
D
A
(G/A)
Guitar
TAB
Bass
TAB
Drums
D.S.1.x only
Perc.
(Shaker)
26
Bb
(Ab/Bb)
Eb
Vocal
With a couple of kids run –ning in the yard – of
Other
Piano
A
(G/A)
D
Guitar
TAB
Bass
TAB
Drums
D.S.1.x only
Perc.
(Shaker)

Vocal
Other
Piano
Guitar
Bass
Perc. Drums
29
Bb/F
to 1. F7
ha ha ha ha
Coda 1.
E7
ha ha ha ha
Des- mond and Mol - ly Jones -
D.S.1.x
A/E
E7
E7
(Wood Block)
(Wood Block)
(Wood Block)
D.S.1.
D.S.2.
ha ha ha ha ha ha  ha  ha  ha ha ha ha ha  ha ha ha  ha  ha ha ha ha ha  ha ha Thank you Ooo  ha ha ha
Coda 2.
Gm
F7
Bb
And if you want some fun,  take Ob -la -di Ob- la -da
F#m
E7
A

312

# While My Guitar Gently Weeps

Words & Music by
**George Harrison**

5
Vocal
Other
Guitar I
Guitar II
Bass
Drums
Perc.
Am
G
D
E
I look
A
Am
Upper part 1x tacet
Am/G
D9/F#
at you all see the love there that's sleep
at the world and I no tice it's turn
at you all see the love there that's sleep
314
( 1x tacet )

FM7
(Upper part 1x tacet)
12
Vocal
- ing
- ing
- ing
While my gui - tar - gent - ly weeps -
While my gui - tar - gent - ly weeps -
While my gui - tar - gent - ly weeps -
Am
G
Other
Guitar I
Guitar II
Bass
Drums
Perc.
D
E
B Am
15
I look - at - the floor -
With eve - ry - mis - take -
Look at - you all -
1H.C 1H.U 1H.U D
H.C D
P
g

18  Am/G   D9/F#   FM7
Vocal
– and – I see – it – needs sweep – ing
– we must sure – ly – be learn – ing
Other
Guitar I
Guitar II
Bass
Drums
Perc.
D.S.x
21  Am   Upper part D.S. only →   G   to   1.   C
Vocal
Still my gui – tar – gent – ly weeps –
Still my gui – tar – gent – ly weeps –
Still my gui – tar – gent – ly weeps –
Other
Guitar I
C ~~~~ D
C ~~~~ D
Guitar II
Bass
Drums
Perc.

(with Repeat)
24
E
C  A
C#m
Vocal
I  don't  know  why  —  —  —
I  don't  know  how  —  —  —
Other
(Piano)
Guitar I
C
C  D
H.C
Guitar II
Bass
H
H
Drums
D.S.x (Tambourine)
Perc.
27
F#m
C#m
Bm
Vocal
no — bo — dy told — you
you — were di — ver — ted
how — to un fold — — your love—
You — were per — ver — ted — too—
Other
Guitar I
Guitar II
Bass
H
Drums
Perc.

I don't know how
I don't know how
some - one con - trolled you
you - were in - ver - ted
They - bought and sold - - you -
No - one al - ert - ed - you -

39
Vocal
Other
Guitar I
Guitar II
Bass
Perc. Drums
E
2.
C
look
look
yeah
I
I
C
C D
g
U D
C
12 12 12
12 12 12 12
12
12
12
13
14 14 14 13
g
14 14
C D
3
3
7 7 7 9 9 9
6 6 6 7 9
3 3 2 3
5 7
S
S
E
D Am
Am/G
D9/F#
ah
H C
Q.C
C
H
1H.C
1H.C
Vib. & D
g
12 14 14
13 13 15 15
13
14
12 14 14 14 14
14
g
H C
Q.C
C
H 1H.C 1H.C
Vib. & D
3
3
3
3
7 7 9 6 7
9 9 9 9 9
7 7 7 5 5 5
7 7 7 4 4 4

FM7
Am
G
D
E
Am
Am/G
D9/F#
Vocal
Other
Guitar I
Guitar II
Bass
Drums
Perc.
(Tambourine)
Vib. & D
8va

54
FM7
Am
G
C
Vocal
Other
Guitar I
Guitar II
Bass
Drums
Perc.
58
E
Coda
C
E
Am
D.S.
(Tambourine)

62
Am/G    D9/F#    FM7    Am
Vocal
oh    oh
oh
Other
Guitar I
C
Guitar II
Bass
Drums
Perc.
66
G    D    E    Am
Vocal
oh    oh    oh
Other
Guitar I
C    D    H
Guitar II
Bass
Drums
Perc.

70
Am/G
D9/F#
FM7
Am
Vocal
Other
Guitar I
Guitar II
Bass
Perc. Drums
Perc.
oh - oh - oh - oh -
74
G
C
E
F
Am
oh - - oh -
323

78
Am/G    D9/F#    FM7    Am
Vocal
oh – – oh – –    oh – oh – –
Other
Guitar I
Guitar II
Bass
Perc. Drums
82
G    D    E    Am
Yeah    Yeah –    Yeah –

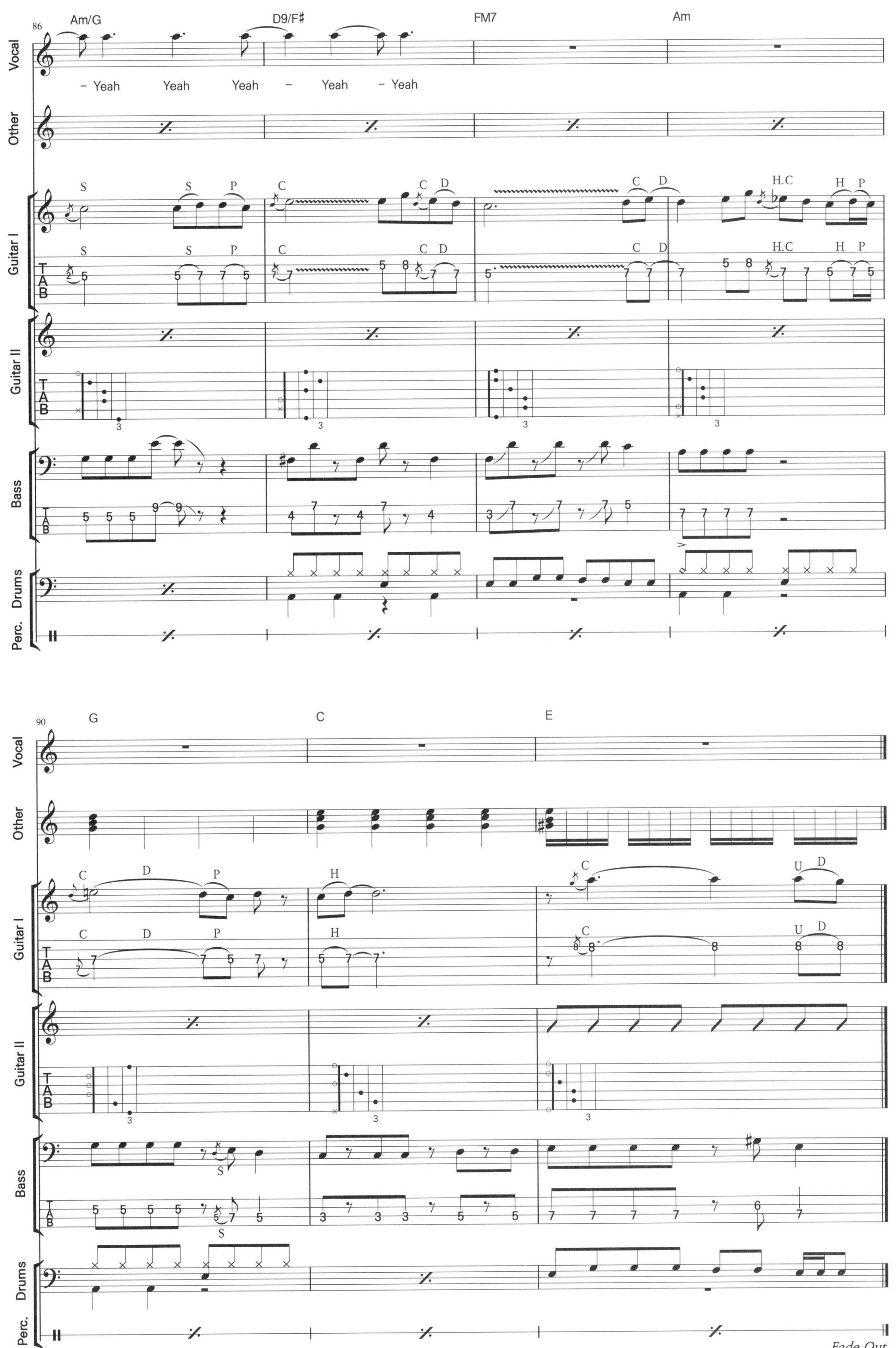
Yeah Yeah Yeah Yeah Yeah
Fade Out

# Birthday

Words & Music by
John Lennon, Paul McCartney

You say it's your birth - day
It's my birth -day too, - yeah
They say it's your birth - day

We're gon - na have a good time
I'm
glad it's your birth - day
Hap - py birth - day to - you

B
25
(N.C.)
Vocal
Other
Guitar I
TAB
Guitar II
TAB
Bass
TAB
Drums
Perc.
29
(N.C.)
Vocal
Other
Guitar I
TAB
Guitar II
TAB
Bass
TAB
Drums
Perc.
330

C
33
E
Vocal
Other
Guitar I
Guitar II
Bass
Drums
Perc.
Yes we're go – in' to a par – ty par – ty
(Hand Clap)
(Tambourine)
37
E
Vocal
Other
Guitar I
Guitar II
Bass
Drums
Perc.
Yes we're go – in' to a par – ty par – ty
Yes we're go – in' to a par – ty par – ty

I would like you to dance - (Birth - day -) Take a
cha - cha - cha - chance - (Birth - day -) I would like you to dance - (Birth - day -) Ooo
(Organ)
(Piano)
Vocal
Other
Guitar I
Guitar II
Bass
Drums
Perc.

48
Vocal
Other
Guitar I
Guitar II
Bass
Drums
Perc.
G
to 1.
E/B
E
dance!
Yeah
(Piano)
8va
W.C
W.C
W.C
51
2.
(N.C.)
Vocal
Other
Guitar I
Guitar II
Bass
Drums
Perc.
U
D
C D
H P
D.S.1.
333

Coda 1.
Coda 2.
Hap - py
birth - day to - you
Slow
D.S.2.
334

# Yer Blues

Words & Music by
John Lennon, Paul McCartney

lo – ne – ly
e – ve – ning
wan – na die –
wan – na die –
If I –ain't dead al–ready–
If I –ain't dead al–ready–
ooh    girl – you know the rea–son why
ooh    girl – you know the rea–son
In the mor – why
My

336

mo - ther was of the sky
ea - gle picks my eye
Black cloud - crossed my mind
My fa - ther was of the earth
The worm he licks my bone -
Blue mist round my soul -
But I am of the u - ni - verse
I feel so - su - i - ci - dal
Feel so - su - i - ci - dal
And
Just like
E - ven
you know what it's worth - -
Dy - lan's Mis - ter Jones - -
I'm lo - ne - ly
Lone - ly
wan - na die - - -
wan - na die - - -
If I
If I

ain't dead al – rea – dy
ooh
girl – you know the rea – son why
The
ain't dead al – rea – dy
ooh
girl – you know the rea – son why
3 times Repeat
hate my – rock and roll – – – wanna die – –
yeah wan – na die –

If I ain't dead al - rea - dy Ooh
girl - - you know the rea - son why
(Dubbing Snare)

28
D E
Vocal
Guitar I
Guitar II
Bass
Drums
Perc.
32
A
E
Vocal
Guitar I
Guitar II
Bass
Drums
Perc.
340

36
G
B7
E
A
Vocal
Guitar I
TAB
Guitar II
TAB
Bass
TAB
Drums
Perc.
39
E/B
B7
E
E
Vocal
Guitar I
8va
Guitar II
TAB
Bass
TAB
Drums
Perc.

42
E
A
Vocal
Guitar I
Guitar II
Bass
Drums
Perc.
45
A
E
Vocal
Guitar I
Guitar II
Bass
Drums
Perc.
342

Vocal
Guitar I
Guitar II
Bass
Drums
Perc.
48
G
B7
(N.C.)
Yes    I'm
D.S.
Coda
51
E    A    E/B    B7    F    E
why         Yes I'm lone-ly         wan - na die -         Yes I'm
Fade Out

# Helter Skelter

Words & Music by
John Lennon, Paul McCartney

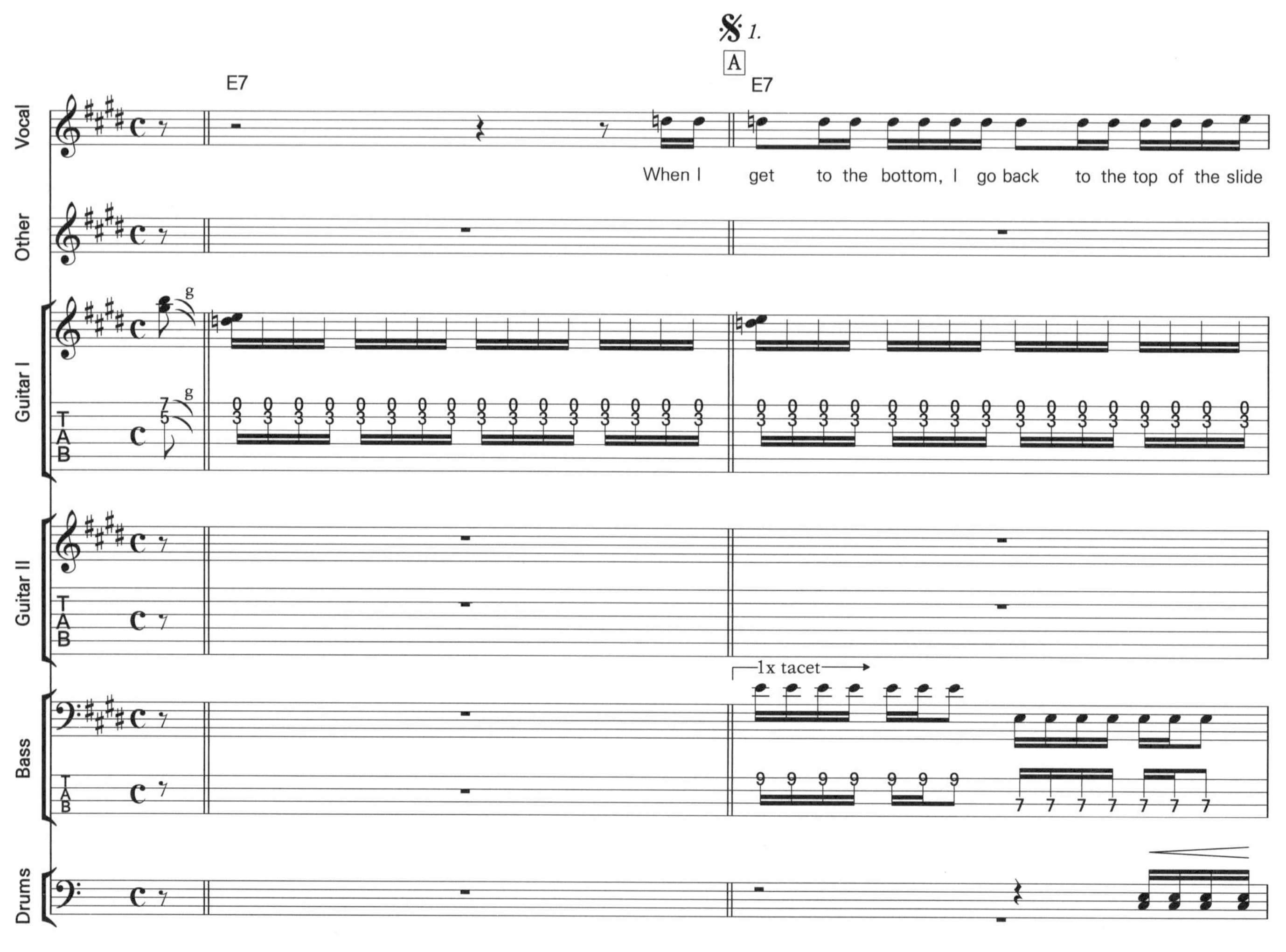

Where I stop and I turn and I go for a ride   Till I get to the bot-tom and I see you a-gain  -
Yeah yeah yeah
D.S.1x
(Chorus)
Yeah
(1x tacet)
(H.H Open)
Do   you   don't   you want - me to love - you
I'm
345

com - ing down fast but I'm mi - les a- bove - you
Tell me, tell me, tell - me, co - me on, tell -
AH
AH
- me the an - swer -
Well, you may be a lo-ver but you ain't no - dan - cer -
Now,
da da da da da da da

C
15
A
E7
A
Hel – ter Skel – ter
Hel – ter Skel – ter
Hel – ter Skel – ter
Vocal
Other
Guitar I
Guitar II
Bass
Drums
18
E7
to 2.
1.
Yeah
Hu – Hu
Well,
2.( Ooh – )
H.C
H.C H.C
U U U U U
g
H.C
H.C H.C U U U U U
g
H
H
H
H
H
H
H

2. (with Repeat)
D
Vocal
Other
Guitar I
Guitar II
Bass
Drums
E7
will you, won't you want – me to make – you
2. (do you don't)
I'm com-ing down fast but don't – let me break – you
( – you–
AH
D.S. 2x only
C
C
C
C
g
H H H H H H
H H H H H
E7
G
A
Tell me, tell me, tell – me the an- swer you may be a lov –er but you ain't no dan –cer
(ain't no dan –
– – )
Feedback
H H H H

Look out, -
Look out,
cause here she comes!
- cer - )
da da da da da da da
AH
-
AH
349

Coda 1.
Coda 2.
E7
When I
Well,
Hel - ter - skel - ter
She's
Yeah
Feedback
(8va)
Vocal
Other
Guitar I
Guitar II
Bass
Drums
D.S.1
D.S.2
E7
com - ing down fast
Yes, she is
Yes, - she is
F

E7
Vocal
Other
Guitar I
Guitar II
Bass
Drums
coming down fast
wu
(Gt.3.)
U D
8va
15 15
15 15
14 14
14
12 12
12 12
E7
Slow
Slide
Slide
8va
20 17 14 12
20 17 14 12
8 5 2 0
8 5 2 0
g
g
3
roll
(Dobbing Tom)

E7
a tempo
G E7
( 2x Fade In )
Vocal
Other
Brass Fake
Guitar I
Feedback
Feedback
12
g
3
Guitar II
Bass
7
0
0
0
H P H
P H H H H
H P H
P H H H H
Drums
45
E7
Vocal
Other
Guitar I
Guitar II
H H H H
P H
H H H H
H H H H
H P H
Bass
7 7 7 7 7 7 7 7 7 7 5 7 5 7
6 7 7 9 7 9 9
5 7 5 7
5 7 5 7 5 7
Drums
48

51
E7
Vocal
Other
Guitar I
Guitar II
Bass
Drums
1.
54
E7
(Brass Fake)
2.
E7
(Brass Fake)
Fade Out
353

57
E7
Vocal
Other
Guitar I
TAB
Guitar II
TAB
Bass
TAB
Drums
60
E7
Slow
( Ringo Shout )
I've got blisters on my fingers !
(Brass Fake)
roll

# Paperback Writer

Words & Music by
John Lennon, Paul McCartney

355

Dear Sir or Ma - dam will you
thou - sand pa - ges, give or
Ah
read my book It took me years to write, - will you take a look? It' - s based on a nov - el by a
take a few; I'll be writ - ing more - in a week or two. I can make it long - er if you
Ah
Ah
Ah
Ah

G7
C
Vocal
man named Lear and I need a job — so I want to be a pa-per-back writ-er —
like the style, I can change it round — and I want to be a pa-per-back writ-er —
Other
Ah Ah Ah
(1x tacet)
Guitar I
Guitar II
3
Bass
S S
S S
Drums

C G7
B G7
Vocal
— pa-per back writ-er. —
— pa-per back writ-er. —
It's a dirt-y sto-ry of a
If you real-ly like — it you can
Other
pa-per back writ-er.
1x tacet
Ah
Guitar I
H
H
Guitar II
3
3
Bass
Drums

357

22
G7
Vocal
dirt – y man, – and his cling – ing wife – – does – n't un – der – stand. His son is work – ing for the
have the rights, – It could make a mil – lion for you ov – er – night. If you must re – turn – it you can
Other
Ah     Ah     Ah     Ah
Guitar I
Guitar II
Bass
Drums

26
G7
C
Vocal
Dail – y Mail; – It's a stead – y job – But he want to be a pa – per – back writ – er –
send it here, – But I need a break – and I want to be a pa – per – back writ – er –
Other
Ah     Ah     Ah
(1x tacet)
Guitar I
Guitar II
Bass
Drums

359

G7
1.
2. G7
Vocal
Other
Guitar I
Guitar II
Bass
Drums
It's a
H
H
H
H
H
12 12 12 12 12 12
10 12 10 12 10 12 10 12
10 12
E
Pa - per - back writ - er
Pa - per - back writ - er
Repeat & F.O.

# Lady Madonna

Words & Music by
John Lennon, Paul McCartney

La - dy - Ma - don - na
child-ren at - your feet
Won - der how you man - age to make - ends meet -
Who finds - the mo - ney
When you pay the rent -
Did you think that mo - ney was -

Vocal
Other
Piano
Guitar
TAB
Bass
TAB
Drums

%1. C Dm7
12
F G A (Chorus D.S.1.time)
pa pa pa pa — pa pa
G7
pa pa pa
hea — ven sent? —
Fri day night — ar- rives — with out — a suit case
Tues — day af - ter-noon — is ne — ver end — ing

3 3 5 5 7 7 7 7
5 5 3 3 2 2 5 5
5 5 3 3 2 2 5 5

C
pa pa pa pa — pa pa
Am7
pa pa — pa pa
Dm7
pa pa pa pa — pa pa
15
Sun — day mor — ning creep —ing like a nun —
Wednes — day — mor—ning pa - pers did – n't come —
Mon — day's child has learned to tie — his
Thurs — day night your stock —ing — need —ed

3 3 2 2 5 5 3 3
5 5 3 3 5 5 2 2 3 3 7 7 5 5 3 3 2 2 5 5

pa pa pa
boot - lace - - -     See how they run     1.La - dy - Ma-don - na
mend - ing - - -     See how they run     2.La - dy - Ma-don - na
ba - by at your breast     Won - ders how you man - age to feed - the rest - -
ly - ing on the bed -     Lis - ten to the mu - sic play - ing in your head - -
(Crush 1x)
(Ride Cym.)

25
E
A    D    A    D    A    D
Vocal
Other
Piano
Guitar
Bass
Drums
S
S
0 0 3 4    0 0 3 4 2
0 0 3 4    0 0 3 4 2
0 0 3 4    0 0 2 2
0 0 3 4    0 0 2 2
1.
F    G    A
28
Dm7    G7
pa pa pa pa  –  pa pa    pa  pa  pa
(Upper Chorus)
(Lower Chorus)
pa    pa    pa    pa    pa
3
g
g
3 3 5 5 7    g
3 3 5 5 7 7 7 7    2 2 3 3 2 2  5 5    5 5 3 3 2 2  5 5

*D.S.1.*

Coda 1.
E7sus4  E7
Vocal
run
Other
Piano
Guitar
Bass
Drums
(Ride Cym.)
D.S.2.
Coda 2.
F    G    A    G/B
ends    meet
H.C.
H.C.
Cm    G/B    A    G/B    Cm    G/B    A
H.C.
H.C.

# Revolution

Words & Music by
John Lennon, Paul McCartney

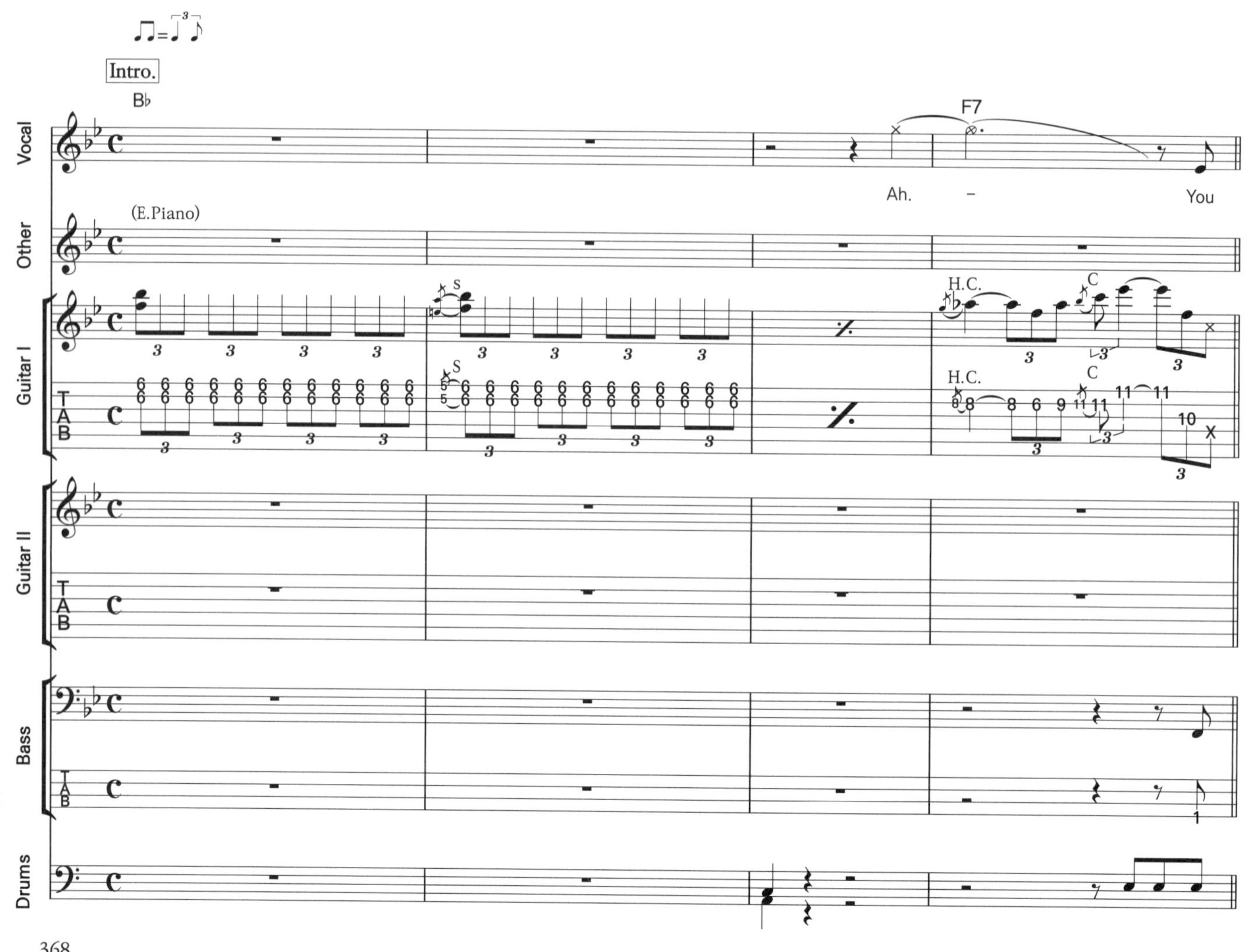

say you want a rev - o - lu - tion, Well you know,
say you got a real so - lu - tion, Well you know,
say you'll change the con - sti - tu - tion, Well you know,

We all want to change the world.
We'd all love to see the plan.
We all want to change your head.

You tell me that it's e - vo - lu - tion, - - - Well -
You ask me for a con - tri - bu - tion, - - - Well -
You tell me it's the in - sti - tu - tion, - - - Well -
- - you know, - - -
- - you know, - - -
- - you know, - - -
We all want - to change the
We're all do - ing what we
You better free - your mind in -

Vocal
Other
Guitar I
Guitar II
Bass
Drums

17
F7
C Cm/G

world.
can.
- stead.

But when you talk a - bout de -
But if you want mo - ney for peo - ple with
But if you go car - ry - ing pic - tures of

H
H
H
H

20
F7
Cm/G
Ab  Bb  G

- struc - tion,
minds that hate,
Chair - man Mao

Don't you know that you can count me out
All I can tell you is, "Bro - ther you have to wait."
You ain't going to make it with a - ny - one a - ny - how.

8va
C C
C C
C C
C C

G
F7
D
Bb
Vocal
Other
Guitar I
Guitar II
Bass
Drums
Don't you know it's gon -na be - al - right,
al - right, -
Eb
Bb
Eb
372

29
Bb
Eb
to
1.
F7
al – right. –
Vocal
Other
Guitar I
Guitar II
Bass
Drums
H
H
H
H
H
3
32
F7
2.
F7
You
Ah –
C D C D C D C D C D
C D C D C D C D C D
H
H
H
H
H
H
H
H
H
H

35
E
Bb
Vocal
Other
Guitar I
Guitar II
Bass
Drums
Ah ah ah ah ah ah ah ah ah ah
38
Eb
F7
Vocal
Other
Guitar I
Guitar II
Bass
Drums
ah ah ah ah ah ah ah ah ah ah ah ah
W.C. W.C. W.C. W.C. W.C. W.C.
D D D D D D

41
F7
Vocal
Other
Guitar I
Guitar II
Bass
Drums
8va
You
D.S.
Coda
44
F7
Al - right, - al - right, -
tr.
W.C. W.U.
W.C. W.U.
F
B♭

47
Vocal
Other
Guitar I
Guitar II
Bass
Drums
Eb   Bb   Eb   Bb
al - right, - al - right, - al - right, - al - right, -
tr.   tr.
H   H
H   H
W.C. W.U.   W.C. W.U.   W.C. W.U.
W.U. W.U. W.U. W.U. W.U.
51
Eb   F   Bb   Cb6   Bb6
al - right, - al - right. -
H P P S
H P P S
W.U   W.U

# Hey Jude

Words & Music by
John Lennon, Paul McCartney

bet – ter
get her
get her
bet – ter
Re – mem – ber to let her in – to your
The min – ute you let her un – der your
Re – mem – ber to let her in – to your
Re – mem – ber to let her un – der your

3. so let it out and let it in 2. Ah

3. Re – mem – ber you let her in – to your
4. Re – mem – ber to let her un – der your

bet – ter

F
Bb

heart then you can start to make it bet – ter Hey
skin then you be – gin to make it bet –
heart then you can start to make it bet –
skin then you'll be – gin to make it bet –
bet –

heart then you can start to make it bet –
skin then you'll be – gin to make it bet –

F
C7
to 2. 1. F
D.S.2.
D.S.2.

(1x tacet)
(1,2x tacet)
(1,2x tacet)

And a - ny - time - you feel the pain - Hey jude - re - frain -
So let it out - and let it in - Hey Jude - be - gin -
Ah -
Don't car - ry the world - up on your shoul - ders - -
You're wait - ing for some - one to - per - form with - -
D.S.1.time (Electric Guitar)
D.S.1.time
1x tacet
1x tacet

15
F7
Bb
Bb/A
Gm
Gm7/F
Vocal
For well you know that it's - a fool - who plays - it cool - - By mark - ing his world-
And don't you know - that it's just you - Hey Jude - you'll do - - The move - ment you need-
Other
Oh -
Piano
Guitar
Bass
Drums
18
C7/E
C7
F
F7
Vocal
- a lit - tle cold - er - - Da da da da - da
- is on - your shoul - der - - Da da da da - da
Other
Piano
Guitar
1x,D.S.1.time
1x,D.S.1.time
Bass
Drums

to Coda 1.
Coda 1.
C7
Vocal
da da da da
da da da da yeah –
Hey –
– Hey – Jude –
Other
Piano
Guitar
Bass
Drums
D.S.1.
D.S.2.
Coda 2.
F
F
C
Yeah yeah, – yeah yeah yeah yeah yeah
1x
Vocal
– ter bet – ter bet – ter bet – ter bet – ter bet – ter oh (Chorus) Da da da
Other
– ter bet – ter bet – ter bet – ter bet – ter bet – ter oh
(Contra Bass)
Piano
Guitar
Bass
Drums
Perc.
(Tambourine)
(Tambourine)
(Hand Clap)

Eb
Bb
F
Vocal
da da da da
Da da da da
Hey - jude -
Other
Piano
Guitar
TAB
Bass
TAB
Drums
Perc.
3times Repeat
F
Eb
Bb
D
2x
Ah - u   Ah - u
Ah - u Ho Da da da -
Da          da       da      da da da da
Da da da da
Hey - Jude
(Strings Section)
Contra Bass Simile
S
S

Vocal
Other
Piano
Guitar
Bass
Drums
Perc.
F
Ju Ju – de Ju – de Ju–de Ju–de Ju–de
F
Ah
Da da da
(Strings) (Horn Section 1.) (Horn Section 2.)
Contra Bass, Strings Section Simile
4times Repeat
E
oh Jude
da da da da
Bb
Da da da da
F
Jude Jude – Jude – Jude Jude Jude
Hey – Jude –
2x
Repeat & F.O.

# Old Brown Shoe

Words & Music by
**George Harrison**

%2.
A C7
C7
Vocal
I want a 1. love that's right — right — is on — ly half of wha — t's
2. pick me up — from where — some try to drag me — do —
D.S.2 love is yours — to miss — that love is some — thing I'd ha —
Organ
Piano
E.Guitar
Bass
Drums
C7
Dm7
wrong —
— wn —
— te —
I want a short — haired girl — who some — times wears it twice as long —
And when I see your smile — re — plac — ing eve — ry thought — less frown —
I'll make an ear — ly start — I'm mak — ing sure that I'm not late —
385

11
Dm7
Vocal
Organ
Piano
E.Guitar
TAB
Bass
TAB
Drums
Now    I'm        step –pin' out   this        old –
Got  me    es  – cap  – ing           from  this        zoo –
For    your   sweet   top      lip   I'm          in –
D.S.2x
D.S.2x
F
3
14
F7
Ab
Ab7
– brown        shoe –
– the         queue –
Ba
Ba
Ba    – by  I'm   in    love  with  you
– by  I'm   in    love  with  you
– by  I'm   in    love  with  you
I'm
I'm
I'm
386

so glad you came – here it won't – be the same – now I'm tell – ing you –
so glad you came – here it won't – be the same – now when I'm with you –
so glad you came – here it won't – be the same – now when I'm with you –
you know you

Vocal
Organ
Piano
E.Guitar
Bass
Drums
2.
B
G
23
1. If I grow up I'll — be a sing — er
D.S.1. I may ap — pear to — b im — per — fect
wear —ing rings on —
my love is some — thing —
3 3
3 3 3 3 3 3
3 7 5 7 5 5
3 3 3 3 7 5 7 5
26
F
G
— eve — ry fin — ger —
— you can't re — ject —
Not wor — ry — ing what they — or you'll — say
I'm chang — ing fast — er — than the wea — ther
3
3
3 3 3 3
3 3 3 3 3 3
1 1 1 1 5 5 1
3 3 3 3 7 5 7 5
1 1 1 1 5 5 1
3 3 3 3 7 5 7 5

29
G
F
F#dim
Vocal
I'll live and love — and may-be some-day who knows ba-by You may com-fort me—
If you — and me should get to—ge—ther who knows ba-by You may com-fort me—
Organ
Piano
E.Guitar
T
A
B
Bass
T
A
B
Drums
to 1.
33
G
G7
C
C7
Heh!
Piano
E.Guitar
T
A
B
Bass
T
A
B
Drums

37
C7
Dm7
Vocal
Organ
Piano
E.Guitar
Bass
Drums
41
Dm7
F
F7
Vocal
Organ
Piano
E.Guitar
Bass
Drums

45
Vocal
Organ
Piano
E.Guitar
Bass
Drums
Ab
Ab7
F
Eaug
3
3
3
3
3
3
3
3
3
3
3
3
8 8 8
8 8 8
8 7 9 7
8 6 5 6 5
6 5 4
3
2
1 1 1
2
2 1
1 3 1
7
11 11 11 15 13 15 13 15 11 11 15 13 15 13 15 11 8 8 12 10 12 10 12 8 7 7 11 9 11 9 11 7
49
Am
Coda 1.
G7
Heh!
I know my
H.C
C
D
3
3
3
3
3
H.C
C
D
7 5 7 7 5 5 5 5 5 8 8 8 5
7
3 3 3
7 5 7 5 3 5 5 2
3 5 2 5 3
3 3 3 3
D.S.1.
D.S.2.

Coda 2.
52
F
Eaug
Am
Vocal
Organ
Piano
E.Guitar
Bass
Drums
so glad you came – here it won't – be the same – now when I'm with you
55
Am
C7
1.2.3.4x tacet
D
Yeah yeah yeah – – – Tu la – Tu ru tu –
1.2.3.4x tacet
1.2.3.4x tacet
1x only
Repeat & F.O.
392

# Don't Let Me Down

Words & Music by
John Lennon, Paul McCartney

Vocal
Keyboard
Guitar I
Guitar II
Bass
Drums
F#m7
F#m7/B
E
A/E
E
D.S.repeat x
Don't let me down. - -
Don't let me
(Hie     Hie -
F#m7
F#m7/B
E
A/E
to
down, - -
Don't let me down, - -

B
1.
E
(Upper part D.S.x tacet)
F#m7
Vocal
Nobody ever loved me like she does — oo she does, — yes, she does.—
and from the first time that she really done me oo she done — me, she done me good.—
Keyboard
Guitar I
Guitar II
Bass
Drums
EM7
Esus4
E
F#m7
And if somebody loved me like she do me, oo she do —
I guess nobody ever really done me, o she done—

16
F#m7
EM7
Esus4
E
3
2.
C
E
Vocal
Keyboard
Guitar I
Guitar II
Bass
Drums
- me, -        yes, she does. -
- me, -        she done me good. -
Don't let me        I'm in love for the first-
Don't let me
S        S
H
H
3        3        3        3
20
E
B7
- time.        Don't you know - it's gon-na  last.        It's a love - that lasts - for-ev-
g        g
g        g
3
396

Vocal
Keyboard
Guitar I
Guitar II
Bass
Drums
24
B7
E
A
E
3
- er,
It's a love - that had - no - past.
Don't let me
D.S.
Coda
D
E
F#m7
28
(Singing Fake)
Hie
Hie

E
F#m7
Ah!
F#m7
E
A
E
Don't let me down.
398

# The Ballad Of John And Yoko

Words & Music by
John Lennon, Paul McCartney

Vocal
Piano
Guitar I
Guitar II
Bass
Perc. Drums
E
- ton, -
- ris, -
- ton, -
- na, -
- don, -
trying to get to Hol - land or Fance. -
hon - ey-moon - ing down by the Seine. -
talk - ing in our beds for a week. -
eat - ing choc' - late cake in a bag. -
fif - ty a - corns tied in a sack. -
The
Pe - ter Brown -
The
The
The
E7
man in the mac - said, "You've got to go back." You know they did - n't ev - en give us a chance. -
- called to say, - "You can make it O. K., You can get mar - ried in Gib - ral - ter near Spain." -
news - peo - ple said, - "Say, what're you do - ing in bed?" I said, "We're on - ly trying to get us some peace." -
news - pa - pers said. - "She's gone to his head; They look just like two Gu - rus in drag." -
men from the press - said "We wish you suc - cess; It's good to have the both of you back." -
400

Christ! You know it ain't ea - sy, - you know how hard it can be -
The way things are go - ing -

they're gon - na cru - ci - fy - me.
me.
Sav - ing up your mo - ney for a
B7
to E
1.2.4.
(5x)
3.
E
B A
Vocal
Piano
Guitar I
Guitar II
Bass
Perc. Drums
gliss

22
A
Vocal
Piano
Guitar I
Guitar II
Bass
Drums
Perc.
rain - y day, - giv - ing all - your clothes to cha - ri - ty.
25
A
B7
Last night the wife said, "Oh boy, when you're dead you don't take no - thing with you but your
3
2 7 6 6 4 6 4

Vocal
Piano
Guitar I
Guitar II
Bass
Drums
Perc.
28
B7
soul." - - Think!
Coda
E
me.
(Maracas)
D.S.
31
C B7
The way things are go - ing - they're gon - na cru - ci - fy -

34
Vocal
Piano
Guitar I
Guitar II
Bass
Perc. Drums
E
B7
me.
37
B7
E
E6
405

# Come Together

Words & Music by
John Lennon, Paul McCartney

Here come old flat – top He come groo – vin' up slow – ly He got Joo, Joo, eye – ball He one
ho – ly rol – ler He got hair down to his knee

Vocal
Keyboard
Guitar I
Guitar II
Bass
Drums
G7
D7(#9)
B
Got to be a jok - er He just do want he please - Shoo
(Stick)
D7(#9)
D7(#9)
C
shoo
shoo
shoo
He wear no shoe shine He got
He Bag Pro - duc - tion He got
He rol - ler coas - ter He got

D7(#9)
Vocal
Keyboard
Guitar I
Guitar II
Bass
Drums
toe jam foot-ball He got mon-key fin-ger He shoot Co-ca Co-la He say,
wal-rus gum-boot He got O-no side-board He one spi-nal cra-cker He got
ear-ly warn-ing He got Mud-dy Wa-ter He one Mo-jo fil-ter He say,
12 12 14 14 12 12 14 12
10 10 10 10 10 10 10 10
A
G7
"I know-you, you know-me" One thing I can tell you is you
feet down be-low - - his knee Hold you in his arm-chair, You can
"One, and one, and one - - is three" Got to be good look-ing 'cause He's
Q.C
Q.C
7 7 9 9 7 7 9 9 7 7 9 9 7 7 9 9
5 5 5 5 5 5 5 5 5 5 5 5 5 5 3
5 5 5 5 5 3

24
G7    Bm    A    to⊕    1.    G    A
Vocal
got    to    be    free –
feel    his    dis – ease –
so    hard    to    see –
Come to – ge – th – er    right    now – –    o – ver me
Keyboard
Guitar I
T A B
Guitar II
T A B
Bass
T A B
Drums

27
2.    G    A    D7(#9)
Vocal
now – –    o – ver me    Shoo    Right –
Keyboard
(E.Piano)
Guitar I
T A B
Guitar II
H
T A B
H
Bass
S    S    H
S    S    H
Drums
(Rim)    6    3    6    3    6    3

D7(♯9)
He come -
A

Coda
now — — o — ver me
shoo shoo shoo oh
D.S.
(Stick)
412

45 F D7(#9)
Vocal
Keyboard
Guitar I
8va
Guitar II
Bass
Drums
Come to - ge - ther, yeah
49 D7(#9)
Come to - ge - ther, yeah
Come to - ge - ther, yeah

53
D7(#9)
Vocal
Come to - ge - ther, yeah
Come to - ge - ther, yeah
Keyboard
Guitar I
57
D7(#9)
Come to - ge - ther, yeah -
Come to - ge - ther, yeah -
Guitar II
Bass
Drums
414

D7(#9)
Vocal
Keyboard
Guitar I
Guitar II
Bass
Drums
Ah
Come to - ge - ther, yeah
C
H.U
C
C
UD P
D P
T A B
15 15
10 12 12 10
13 13
13 13 13 13 10
D P
S
10 10 10 10
10 10 10 10
10 12
10
12
12
10 10 9 10 10
S
D7(#9)
Come to - ge - ther, yeah
Come to - ge - ther,
C
UD P
C
13 13
13 13 10
13 13
12
10 10 10 10 10 10 10
10 10 10 10 12
12 10 10 10 10
10 12
10
10 10 10 10 10 10 10 10 10 10
Fade Out

# Something

Words & Music by
**George Harrison**

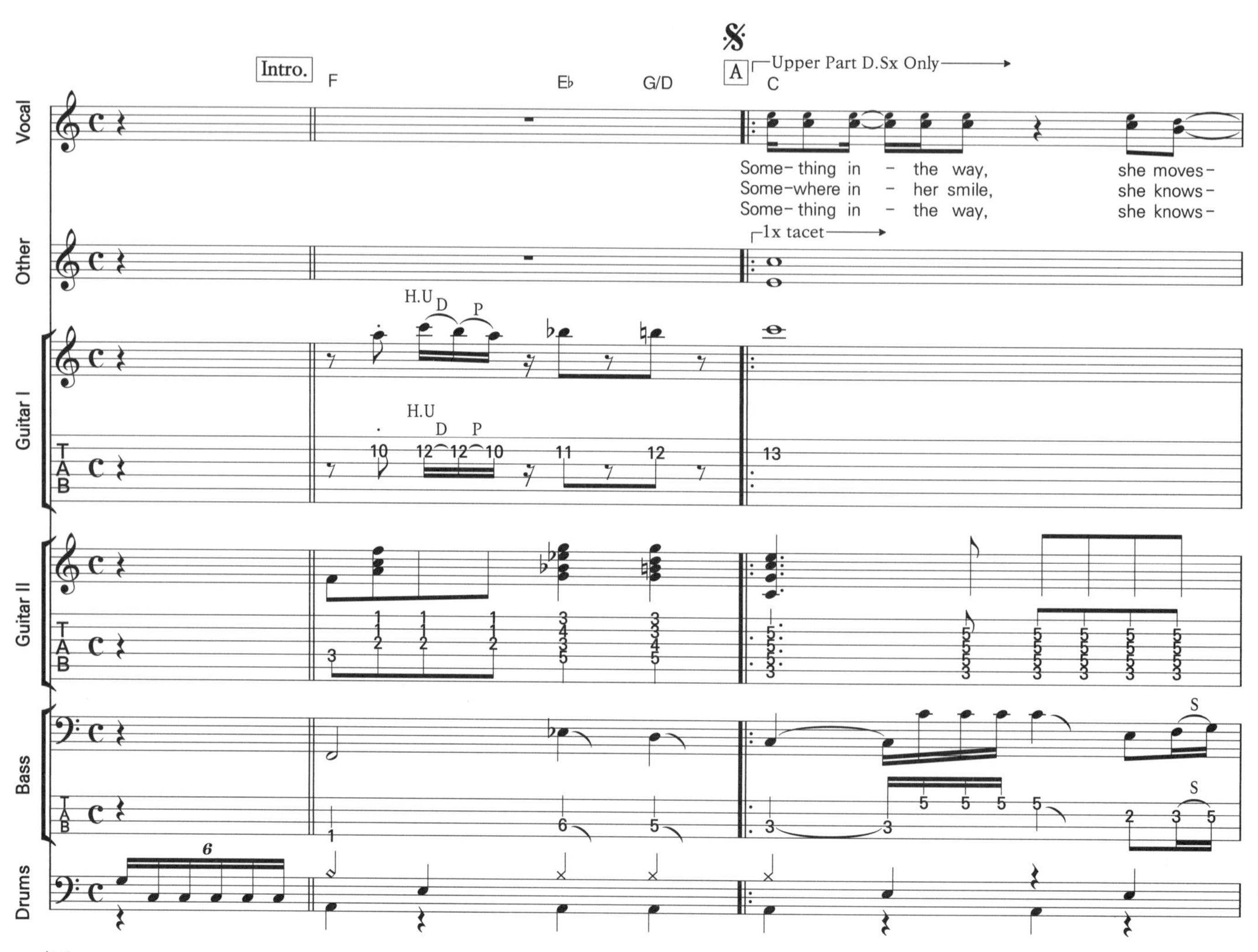

CM7
C7
At - tracts - me like no oth - er lov -
That I - don't need no oth - er lov -
And all - I have - to do - is
F
D7
(Upper Part D.Sx Only)
- er
- er
think of her
Some - thing in - the way, she - woos -
Some - thing in - her style, she - shows -
Some - thing in - the things, she - shows -

418

You're ask - ing me - will my - love grow I don't know - - - I - - don't
know You stick a - round - now it may show I don't know -

Vocal
Other
Guitar I
Guitar II
Bass
Drums
19
D
G
C
C
C
CM7
– – – I – – don't know
23
C7
F
D
G7
(E.Guitar)

421

# Octopus's Garden

Intro.
Vocal
Other
Guitar I
Guitar II
Bass
Drums
E
C#m
A
B
(Piano)
1x tacet
2x only
A
E
C#m
A
I'd like to be — un – der the sea — In an oc – to – pus's gar – den in the shade –
We would be warm — be – low the storm — In our lit – tle hide away — be-neath the waves –
We would shout — and swim a – bout — The co – ral that lies — – be-neath the waves–
Ooo –
Ooo –

He'd let us in — knows where we've been — In his
Rest -ing our head — on the sea bed — In an
Oh, what joy — for eve - ry girl and boy —
Ah Ah Ah — — — Ah Ooo — Ooo —
oc - to - pu - s's gar - den in the shade —
oc - to - pu - s's gar - den near a cave
Know - ing they're hap - py and they're safe
I'd ask my friends to
We would sing and
We would be so
2. Ah Ah Ah — — — Ah
3. Hap — py and they're safe
(1x tacet)

come and see – –
dance a – rou – nd
hap – py you and me –
An oc – to – pu – s's gar – den with me –
Be – cause we know we can't be found
No one there to tell us what to do –
I'd like to be – un – der the sea, – In an oc – to – pu- s's gar – den in the shade–
D.S. time only
Ah – Ah

20
Vocal
Other
Guitar I
Guitar II
Bass
Drums
1.
2.
(S.E. Voice)
E
E
D A
Ah
Ah
(E.Guitar)
8va
23
F#m
D
Ah
Ah
Ah
8va

427

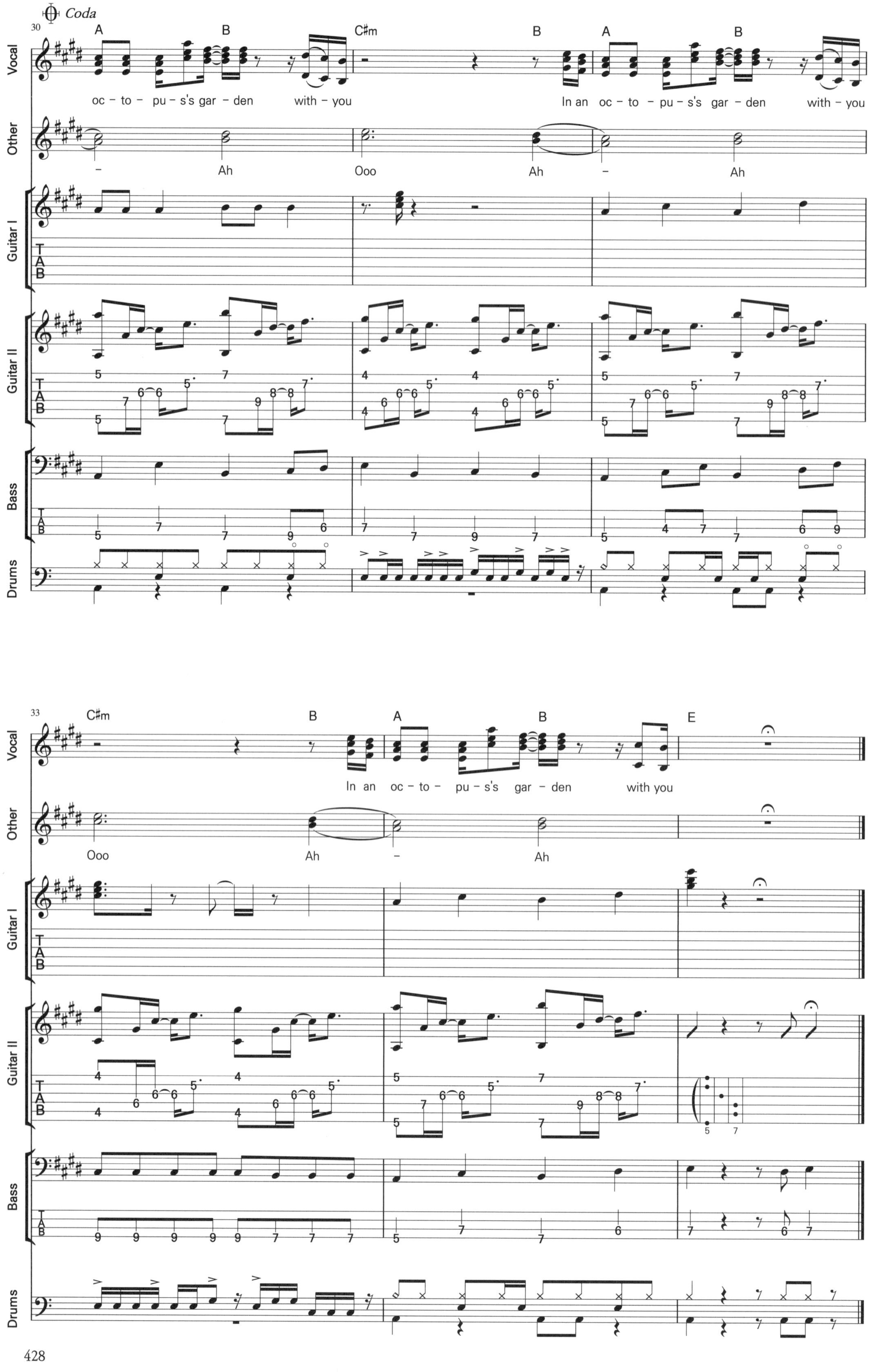
Coda
30
A
B
C♯m
B
A
B
Vocal
oc – to – pu – s's gar – den with – you
In an oc – to – pu – s's gar – den with – you
Other
– Ah Ooo Ah – Ah
Guitar I
Guitar II
Bass
Drums
33
C♯m
B
A
B
E
Vocal
In an oc – to – pu – s's gar – den with you
Other
Ooo Ah – Ah
Guitar I
Guitar II
Bass
Drums

# Here Comes The Sun

Words & Music by
**George Harrison**

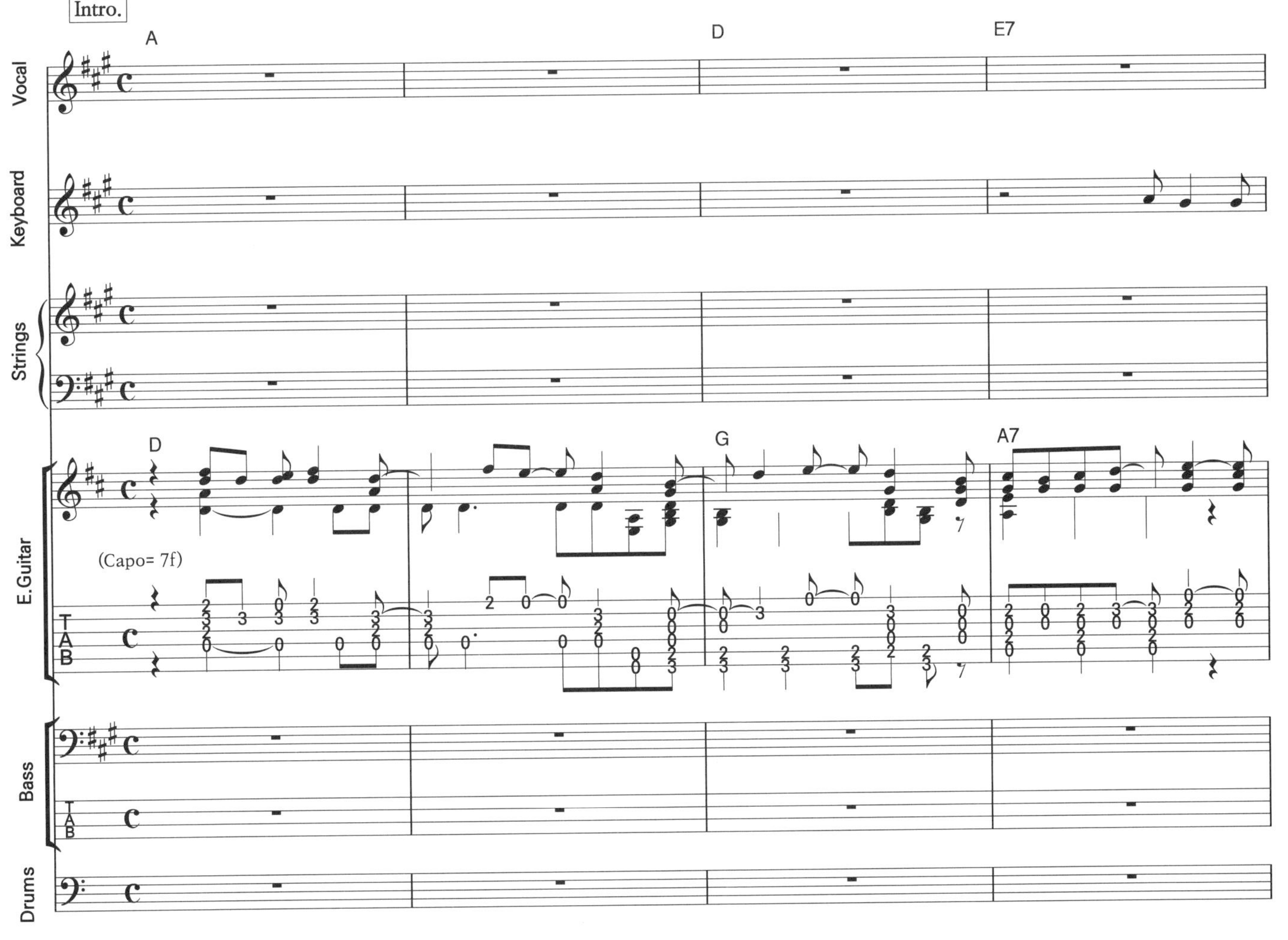

430

It's all - right
1. Lit - tle dar - ling
2. Lit - tle dar - ling
3. Lit - tle dar - ling
2x
It's been - a - long - cold - lone - ly win - ter
The smiles - re - turn - ing - to - their fac - es
I feel - that - ice - is - slow - ly melt - ing

431

Vocal
Keyboard
Strings
E.Guitar
Bass
Drums
20
A
D
Lit - tle dar - ling
Lit - tle dar - ling
Lit - tle dar - ling
It feels - like - years - since it's - been here
It seems - like - years - since it's - been here
It seems - like - years - since it's - been clear
2x
D
G
23
E7
A
Here comes - the sun - do do do do
A7
D
432

Here comes - the sun, - and I - say "It's all - right"

Vocal
Keyboard
Strings
E.Guitar
Bass
Drums
2.
E7
C
G
D
A7
F
C
G
A
E7
C
G
Sun,
sun,
3.4x
D
A7
F
C
(Synth.) 1x tacet

1.2.3.4.
Vocal
sun, here it comes – – –
Keyboard
Strings
3.4x
2.4x
(Synth.)
(Synth.)
G
D
A7
E.Guitar
TAB
Bass
TAB
Drums
5.
A
E7
Esus4
Vocal
comes – – –
Keyboard
Strings
D
A7
Asus4
E.Guitar
TAB
Bass
TAB
Drums

Coda
Here comes — the sun —
— do do do do
Here comes — the sun,

"It's all - right"
"It's all - right"
rit.- - - - -
437

# Across The Universe

Words & Music by
John Lennon, Paul McCartney

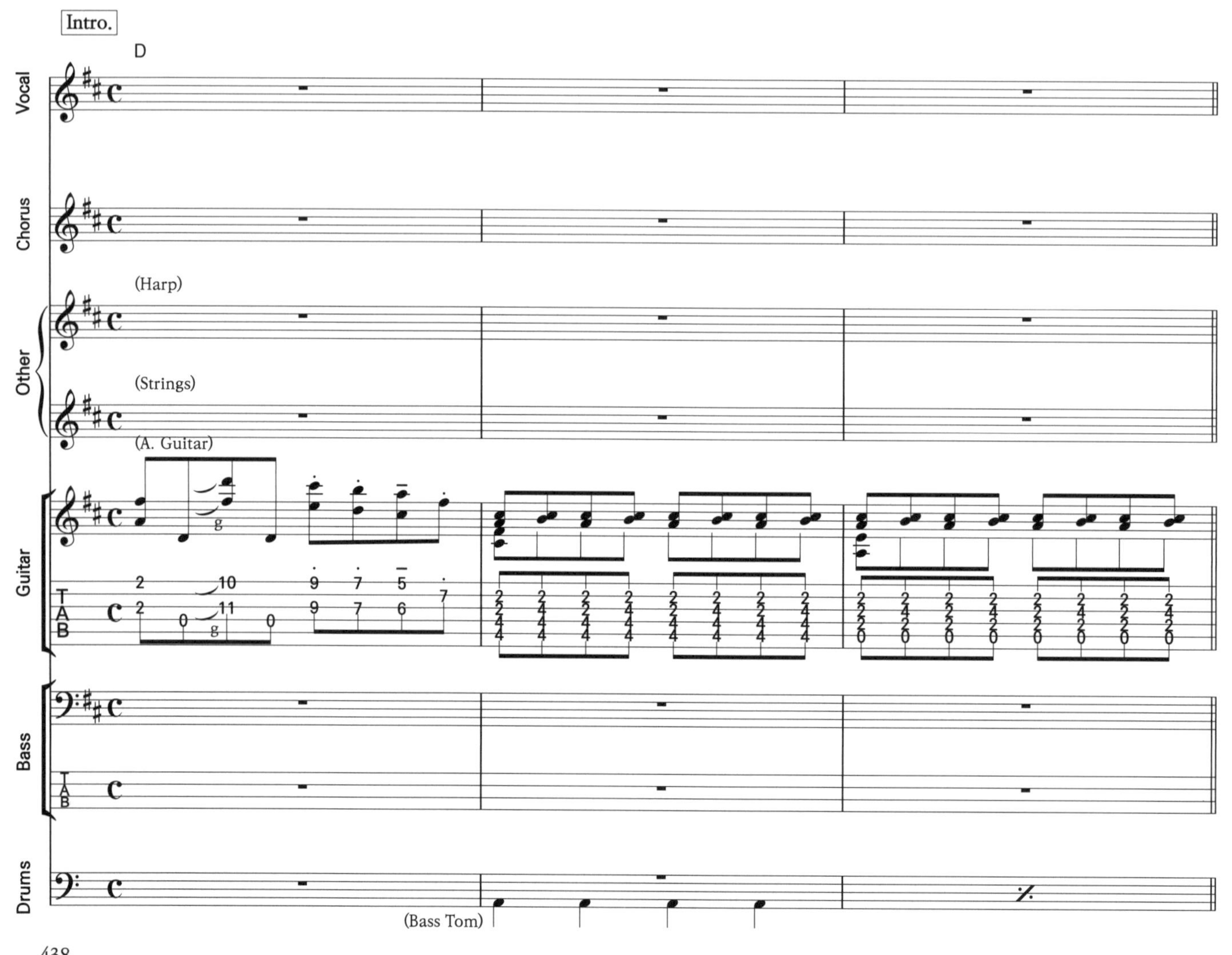

A
D    Bm    F#m    Em7
Words are flow-ing out - like end-less rain in-to a pa-per cup, They slith-er while - they pass they slip a-way-
Vocal
Chorus
Other
Guitar
TAB
Bass
Drums
A7    D    Bm    F#m
- a-cross the u-ni-verse -    Pools of sor-row waves of joy - are drift-ing through my o-pen mind, pos-

Vocal
Chorus
Other
Guitar
Bass
Drums
Em7
Gm
B
D
- sess - ing and ca - ress - ing me. -
Jai - Gu - ru - - De - va -
fp
3
3
5
3
A7
A
Om
No - thing's gon - na change my world -
3
5
7
3
(Maracas)
440

No-thing's gon-na change my world -
No-thing's gon-na change my world -
No-thing's gon-na change my world -
Im-ag-es of bro-ken light which dance be-fore me like a mil-lion

eyes, they call me on and on a - cross the u - ni - verse, -
Thoughts me - an - der like a rest - less wind-
- in - side a let- ter box They tum -ble blind -ly as they make their way a - cross - the u - ni - verse -

31
D
A7
Jai - Gu - ru - - De - va - Om        No - thing's gon - na change my world -
35
A7        G        D        A7
- No-thing's gon - na change   my world -        No-thing's gon - na change   my world -
Vocal
Chorus
Other
Guitar
Bass
Drums
3        3        3        5        3        3
5 5 5   5 5 5 5        5 5 5 5 5 5 5 5        3 3 3 3 3 3 3 3        5 5 5 5 5 5 5 5        5 5 5 5 5 5 5 5

No - thing's gon - na change my world -
Sounds of laugh - ter shades of earth - are
ring - ing through my o - pen views - In - cit - ing and in - vit - ing me. -
Lim - it - less - un - dy - ing love which

47
F#m    Em7    A7
Vocal
shines a – round me like a mil – lion suns, and calls me on and on a – cross the u – ni – verse –
Chorus
Other
Guitar
Bass
Drums
2.
50
D    D
Vocal
Jai – Gu – ru – De – va – Jai – Gu – ru – De – va –
Chorus
Other
Guitar
Bass
Drums
Repeat & F.O.

# Let It Be

Words & Music by
John Lennon, Paul McCartney

A
Vocal
C G Am FM7 F6 C G
find my – self – in times – of trou – ble Moth-er Ma – ry comes – to me S – peaking words of wis – dom, Let it be–
in my hour of dark – ness She is stan-ing – right in front – of me S – peaking words of wis – dom, Let it be–
Other
Piano
Guitar
TAB
Bass
TAB
Drums
1.
F C
2.
F C
B Am C/G
– – And – – Let it be – let it be – let it be –
(Organ)
8va

let it be -
Whis-per words - - of wis dom   let it be - -
And
when the bro - ken - heart - ed peo - ple   Liv-ing in - the world - - a- gree
when the night - is   cloud - y   There is   still a light - - that shines on me
There will   be (an)ans - wer   let it be -
Shine un - till to-mor - row   let it be -
1x tacet

17
F    C    G    Am    F
For though they may - be part - ed    There is    still a chance - that they - will see - -
I    wake    up    to    the sound - of mu - sic    Mo-ther Ma - ry comes - to me -
Vocal
Other
Piano
Guitar
2x only
H    S    H
H    S    H
TAB
Bass
(1x tacet)
(1x tacet)
Drums
20
C    G    F    C    Am    C/G
D
There    will    be (an)ans - wer    let it be - -    Let it    be -    let it be -    let it be -
Speak -ing words of    wisdom    let it be - - - - -    Let it    be -    let it be -    let it be -
(1x tacet)    8va
2x only
2x only
S
S
(1x tacet)

let it be -
let it be -
yeah There will be (an)ans - wer let it be - -
There will be (an)ans - wer let it be - -
Let it be
- let it be let it be - - let it be - Whis -per words - of wisdom let it be-
(Brass)

450

29
F  C  F F  C/E G7/D C  B♭ F/A G  F  C
Vocal
(E.Piano)
Other
Piano
8va bassa
Guitar
C
C
T A B
Bass
T A B
3 2 0 3 5 5 5 5 5 3 2 0 3 3 2 0 3 3
Drums
32
F  C  G F C  G C  G
Vocal
(Organ)
Other
Piano
8va
Guitar
H  H
T A B
3 5 3 7 7 5 3 5 5 3 5 3 5
H  H
Bass
T A B
3 5 5 3 5 5 5 5 3 3 2 3 5 5
Drums

35
Am F C G F C
Vocal
Other
Piano
Guitar
Bass
Drums
38
C G Am F C G
Vocal
Other
Piano
Guitar
Bass
Drums
452

Let it be - let it be yeah let it be - - yeah - let it be -
Whis - per words - of wisdom let it be - - - And - - - - Let it be -

let it be    let it be    yeah let it be    Whis-per words  of wis - dom    let it be
(Brass)
(E.Piano)
454

# The Long And Winding Road

Words & Music by
John Lennon, Paul McCartney

Ab  Gm  Cm  Fm  Bb7  Db/Eb
Vocal
Other
Strings
Other
Piano
Bass
Drums
will nev-er dis-ap-pear
I've seen that road be-fore —
(Chorus)
Ab  Gm  Cm  Fm  Bb7
It al-ways leads — me here
lead me to your door—
(Chorus)

The 1. wild and wind – y night – that the rain –
2.3. still they lead me back – to the long – – –
washed a – way –
wind – ing road –
has left a
You left me stand –
(Horns)
1x tacet
8va bassa
Eb  Cm  Ab/Bb
Eb  Eb7  Ab  Ab/Bb  Gm

pool of tears –
– ing here –
crying for the day –  –  –  –
a long – long time – a – go  –  –  –  –
Why leave me stand – ing here,
Don't leave me wait – ing here,
3. keep
let me know – the way –
lead me to your door –

Man - y times - I've been a - lone and man - y times - I've cried - -
An - y way you'll ne - ver know the man - y ways - I've tried - and
(Strings)
459

30
Eb/G    Fm    Bb7    Eb/Bb    Ab
Vocal
Other
Strings
Other
(Strings)
Piano
Bass
Drums
D.S.
but
Coda
33
Fm    Bb7    Eb    Ab/Bb    Eb
Vocal
lead me to your - door        - Yeah yeah yeah yeah -
Other
Strings
Other
Piano
Bass
Drums

# Get Back

Words & Music by
John Lennon, Paul McCartney

A
Vocal
Jo Jo was a man who thought — he was a lon — er But — he knew it could — n't last —
Sweet Lor — et — ta Mar — tin thought — she was a wom — an But — she was an — other — man —
Other
Guitar I
Guitar II
Bass
Drums
A
Jo — Jo left his home in Tuc — son Ar — i — zo — na for —
All — the girls a — round her say — she's got it com — ing but —

Vocal
Other
Guitar I
Guitar II
Bass
Drums
D
A
B
A
- some Cal - i - for - nia grass -
- she gets it while she can -
Get back - !
Get back
C
U
D
g
A
D
A
G/A
D/A
- ! Get back - to where you once be - longed - Get back -
g
g
463

Get back - ! Get back - ! Get back - to where you once be - longed - Get back JoJo !
Get back Loretta !

25
A
D
Go home
Vocal
Other
Guitar I
Guitar II
Bass
Drums
28
A
G
D
C
A
Get back - !
Get back - !
Back -
H.C
C
Vocal
Other
Guitar I
Guitar II
Bass
Drums

to where you once be - longed -
Get back - !
Get back -
- !
Back - to where you once be - longed -
Get back Joe

D
38
Vocal
Other
Guitar I
Guitar II
Bass
Drums
A
D
8va
3
6
g
41
A
G/A
D/A
A
4
H
H
467

Go home    Ah, Get back — !    Yeah, Get back—
— !    Get back — to where you once    be - longed —    Yeah, Get back—

470

Get back!
Get back–

Get back - to where you once be-longed - Ah Get back-
--! Get back - - ---!
Fade Out